A Hand-held Series for the Wife
Serious about Her Marriage

Cinderella, You Lied to Me.
"Where Is the Fairy-tale Effect?"

Adrienne Swearingen

PublishAmerica
Baltimore

First printing

ISBN: 1-4137-6408-8
PUBLISHED BY PUBLISHAMERICA, LLLP
www.publishamerica.com
Baltimore

Printed in the United States of America

Paraphrases and comments regarding Cinderella are only the author's personal view of a spiritual revelation given about this story of a woman after God's own heart.

If ye abide in me, and my words abide in you, ye shall ask what you will and it shall be done unto you.
(John 15:7)

You obey and serve God.
He will honor your obedience by serving you.

Contents

Dedication

This book is dedicated to God, for God's people.

This book is dedicated to my husband, Michael; for without you going through the test and trials with me, this book would have never been. Thank you for being a man who knew how to fight against all that Satan tried to whip you down with. Through steadfast prayer, I watched you submit your will and surrender your heart to God, eventually allowing Him to take over the battle when you realized it was no longer yours to fight. God bless you for being you. Myke & Adrienne, strong and true forever.

To my children, Michael II and DeNaya, for being strong and enduring the tough times with us as they grew up, and for not being impatient and unkind, even when the circumstances seemed to overwhelm the entire family.

DeNaya, thank you for bending your ear to listen as I bounced ideas and plans off of you. Thank you for your love, encouragement and support. I love you, my dear and precious daughter. You are truly a blessing to me and a gift from God.

To my son, Myke II, thanks for showing me that a young man can grow up tough, endure trying and difficult situations and not lose his joy or strength, but that he can keep fighting until he pushes his way through. Thanks for not using women to help you through, taking each trial as it came along, making your way while God prepares you for that special woman. I love you, son.

This book is also dedicated to my spiritual covering and guide. He is my Pastor, Dr. Kerwin B. Lee. I thank him for his willing, supportive and encouraging attitude, as I continually poured information over his e-mail and answering machine regarding goals I wanted to accomplish with the wives at the Berean Christian Church. Pastor, you always say, "What's in you has to come out of you," and because of your teaching, God was able to bring out of me anxiety. He was also able to bring out of me this book, which I dedicate to wives everywhere. Pastor Lee, your style is practical, plain to understand and humorous, but your gift of spiritual wisdom and insight is by no means a laughing matter.

The Author

Adrienne Swearingen was born and raised in Youngstown, Ohio, by her parents, Albert Neal and the late Anne Neal Brown. Adrienne married at the tender age of nineteen years to her husband, Michael. They have successfully reared two children into adulthood, DeNaya, and Michael II.

Adrienne is a licensed & independently ordained Minister called to the office of Prophet (Ephesians 4:11) in her service to God. She is a member of the Berean Christian Church in Stone Mountain, Georgia, under the leadership of Pastor Kerwin B. Lee. Upon joining this ministry, Adrienne organized The Becoming Virtuous Women's Ministry for youth-aged girls. Adrienne and her husband, Michael, serve as coordinators over The Couples Fellowship Ministry. Adrienne continues to teach, individually and in conjunction with her husband, inspirational scripture-based classes to couples in workshops, School of Ministry, and conferences. As God began to burden Adrienne's heart to the pain and challenges many wives suffer through in trying to understand their role in marriage, God allowed Adrienne's pastor to see her vision in starting a ministry for wives at Berean. Adrienne serves as the coordinator of this spirit-filled ministry, entitled "Married Women of Virtue."

Adrienne is also the founder and organizer of The Holy Matrimony Prophetic Ministries. This ministry serves the spiritual needs of the married woman and married couples. This ministry is

PROPHETESS ADRIENNE SWEARINGEN

dedicated to training and equipping married women/couples in practical life skills and character building. Through biblical instruction and personal experience, Adrienne is able and qualified to lecture and teach wives to depend on God and to live a life of virtue as described in Proverbs 31:10-31.

Adrienne's mission is motivating others to keep moving in their relationships with Christ and the vision He has placed in them. She says, "God gives us the power and strength through Jesus Christ to endure all things. We must simply just trust Him."

Adrienne received her call to preach in 1995 and accepted that call to teach and preach the word of God under the pastoral care of Dr. Kerwin B. Lee in December of 2002.

Her favorite scripture comes from the book of Proverbs:

> *Trust in the Lord with all thine heart, lean not unto*
> *thy own understanding. In all your ways*
> *acknowledge Him and He shall direct thy path.*
> *(Proverbs 3:5-6)*

This passage reminds us that in all of our ways, we must trust God. We cannot see our future as God sees it, this scripture calls us into the obedience of trusting Him and acknowledging the fact that He knows what is best for us even in the discomfort of life's circumstances, and we must not continue walking in the way that we see as best but take orders and instructions from heaven.

Foreword

As a graduate student in seminary school, I have many memories of class time. One thing I remember is that for every class, there were two types of reading material. The first was required reading and the second was optional reading. There was a major difference between these two types of readings.

The difference was that the required readings were books that each student had to have and read. On the other hand, the optional reading materials were books that were not mandatory but that could be purchased if the student wanted them. It was always vital for students to have the books that were required because they prepared you to pass the course.

This book *Cinderella, You Lied to Me* should be required reading for every person who is married or desires to get married. Just as the required books in seminary school helped me pass each course, this book will assist readers to pass the test and trials of Holy Matrimony. Adrienne shares real life and personal experiences coupled with biblical principles to convey that marriage is more factual than fairytale.

An investment into this resource will not just benefit Adrienne Swearingen, it will benefit you, sharing with you practical ways to be a godly spouse. It will benefit families by imparting wisdom that is applicable and helpful to family units. It will also help society to raise more couples committed to staying together and working through the highs and lows of marriage.

Remember! *Cinderella, You Lied to Me* is required reading. The sooner you read it and apply it to your life, the sooner you position yourself to pass any marital test, quiz or exam that will come your way.

God bless you, Adrienne, on a job well done!

Dr. Kerwin B. Lee, Senior Pastor
Berean Christian Church
Stone Mountain, Georgia

Introduction

By purchasing this book you have indicated that you like so many other married couples in the world and in the church are admitting that it is hard to hold it all together and you need some help. Holy Matrimony Prophetic Ministries was originally founded to increase the strength of the married woman and help her seek God's perfection in an imperfect marriage, I came to realize that once the wife begins to heal, the couple must be brought together and trained in the direction that God planned so that the marriage as a whole unit can heal. However without instruction in God's Word the marriage will never seem to have purpose. So many couples who build their marriages on the foundations of this world never really understand while even after 30, 40 and sometimes even 50 years of marriage they never really have found happiness.

I like to say this is the book written for a woman that every man should read, because until the man understands the heart of a woman he will never truly be able to make her happy. A man needs to understand the emotional side of a woman. He needs to be taught to care for the emotional needs of his wife catering to her inner, outer, and spiritual side.

I have been writing my ideals down for many years regarding marriage, especially as I have journeyed through my own 27 years of marriage. This is however the first time God has given me the boldness to step out and take the information He has placed within me and share it with an audience through publication. I have supported, encouraged and counseled women regarding marriage for many years, but most recently I have begun to step out and lead a wives support group in my church for wives.

As stated in the writer's introduction my goal for wives is dedicated to training and equipping married women in practical life skills and character building. My goal is to teach them to become a woman of virtue, to hold up and support their husband as he struggles with God's will for his life but never forget that she has a place in life and a purpose as well.

Cinderella You Lied To Me. Where Is The Fairy Tale Effect? Is the first in a handheld series which will be made available to strengthen wives, my prayer is that this series will do in the spirit of wives all God has ordained.

Preface

"Help has arrived"

Does this sounds like your knight in shining armor has arrived or your ship has come in? Well that is exactly what has happened only his name is Jesus. He has sent information from Heaven down to help you grasp an understanding of how you are to operate in your marriage as a helpmate and wife.

The information in this book is designed to heal the mind, and strengthen the heart of the married woman. The information in the chapters is centered on the characteristics and lifestyle of the virtuous woman as described in Proverbs 31:10-31. This book will teach us how the virtuous woman developed her character, maintained her strength, attended to the needs of her household, and developed herself personally, the way God originally desired and planned.

Exodus 10: 7-11 shows us that even King Pharaoh recognized that if he freed the whole family from bondage, we would worship the Lord. Therefore he decided the men could go free but the wife and the children would stay captive. Could this mean that in all actuality the man is free while the woman is not? Is it at all possible that it is the woman who is still in Egypt? That is something to think about as a wife isn't it?

This book will teach us to focus on ourselves and not just our husbands so that the entire family can be free to serve and worship the Lord. I think it is so sad when the world offers more to the married woman than the church offers. The world offers beauty and nail salons, lingerie shops, women's health clubs, body and bath shops along with glamorous 1 day clothing sales. The world is catering to your outer appearance and entices you to spray your body up and down with perfumes to cover the unappealing scent that surrounds you because of your unpleasant attitude about life and your inability to be happy.

The world's desire is that you will believe that if you maintain an attractive weight, keep your hair spiffed up, dress nice and come to bed in sexy lingerie you will satisfy your husband's needs and find complete satisfaction in life. Allow me to be the first to say to you, "That is a lie from the pits of hell." I have come to suggest to you that unless the inner woman, the spirit is catered to then nothing you do to make someone else happy will make you happy. Not even your husband.

You must first become pleasing to yourself before you can please anyone else. The helpmate is continually trying to please everyone else, the children, the husband, the dog and she almost never makes any effort to please herself. Many of you who are reading this book on today honestly think that if your children are happy and your husband is happy then you will be happy and that is not so. You have not filled the void that lies so deep within your heart.

The helpmate, the wife has been too long neglected. Satan attacks your spirit often making you think you have not done enough, you need to do more. His mission is to make every attempt to wear you down. The female is genetically made by God to be the weaker vessel, but she is also called to be the helpmate, which means God ordained you to be solid support for the husband and children. Satan recognizes this and completely understands that if he can drain your strength he can very easily topple the entire family leaving everyone open for his surprise attack.

My goal is to share with you through spiritual insight, wisdom, knowledge, understanding and faith, how God wants to work for you in your marriage. God's plan is that your heart, your mind and your marriage be healed. As you read the remaining chapters, and

CINDERELLA, YOU LIED TO ME.

complete this book my prayer is that it will have helped you discover ways to cater to your spirit, show your husband how to be a better lover to you, help you to get beyond the small arguments, teach you how to stay in an unsuccessful marriage and let the teaching and instruction of God's Word show you how to make it successful. We will discuss how you can better understand what you have asked God to do when you welcomed Him into your home to fix your marriage. We will try to help you understand why your level of pain increased when it was your husband who you prayed that God would fix. We will teach you that it is okay to cry over your marriage. It is your ministry. We will teach you to stand still and know who God really is when you feel you have done all you can. We will teach you that you are not alone when you feel abandoned and living alone while your husband is in the next room. We will discuss with you that Delilah may come into your marriage, but she doesn't have to ruin it. We will teach you that turning to another man when your husband has hurt you is not the route or direction of the Holy Scriptures.

Finally our hope and prayer is that we can introduce you to a wonderful counselor named Jesus and that the only thing He charges you is to lead an obedient life to the word of God. He only ask that you would trust and believe that he is who he says he is and that once you begin to obey the word of God completely, nothing that you ask for will be held back from you. Help has arrived.

"He Won't Flush the Toilet"
Getting Beyond the Trivial

As I continue to lead married women in this assignment God placed in my life, I hear more and more, "Adrienne, you don't understand," and I say over and over again, "Yes, I do. I really do."

When you look at my husband and me now, you see us working for the Lord, serving others and trying to be an example of what a marriage should look like in God's eyes, but I can honestly say to you that what you see now is not a picture of what we looked liked several years ago. We were lost, knee deep in sin and on our way to hell. We did not have a bad marriage and we did our best to honor our commitment to each other; as much as the Devil would allow us anyway, but we had our share of problems and arguments over things that we now realize didn't matter then and still now don't matter now; little things that we would let ruin a whole evening or day, little things that we allowed the enemy to attack us with that would cause us not to speak for several days and be proud of it.

This is where "He Won't Flush the Toilet" comes from. I want to help you understand in this chapter that the plan of the enemy is to destroy and weaken your marriage over small matters so that you will not have any fight left in you when the big things come.

Satan's desire is to bring sin into your home. We were in sin because this word tells us that anger resides in the heart of a fool and a fool does not know Jesus, and we were angry with each other over small things, things like him not flushing the toilet or me not turning a light out or shutting a door. When Satan controls your home, you will go to bed not speaking and not touching over these type of petty issues.

*Don't sin by letting anger control over you. Don't let
the sun go down while you are still angry.
(Ephesians 4:26)*

How many of us have done that in marriage? I think at one time or another we all have and it's sin. It's us letting the evil power of Satan rule our hearts and control us. It's sin, and we feel the power of the enemy using us when we do it, because normally when were so mad that we go to bed without speaking, we're fuming, we're pouting, and we realize if we say one word to each other, we will explode again. That's sin, and we need to realize right now that whenever we become that angry with anyone, we have just slipped into sin. We have just slipped into darkness, a place that the power of God does not go.

My question is: "What can make us that angry?" How can we let the power of the enemy enter our hearts—these Christian hearts—so strong, so boldly, that he controls us so completely in such a manner as this?

My husband laughed at this title, and it is a funny title, but it should make you think. It made me think when I typed it out. But it came about because I realized one day when I was in the bathroom brushing my teeth that the smallest things can make us argue.

We have dual sinks in our bathroom and I looked over at my husband's sink one morning after he had left for work and it was a mess. He had left his deodorant, the toothpaste and several other little items everywhere and I thought to myself, "Now that's just nasty and trifling. Why couldn't he put those things away?" Then I looked at my area and I had makeup, hairpins and other toiletries everywhere on my side of the sink. So I said to myself, "I will clean mine up, leave his a mess, and tell him about it when he gets home." At that moment, the Holy Spirit spoke to me and said, "Hey helpmate, hey support system, maybe he was tired, maybe he was running late, like you did the other morning. Why don't you just clean it up and not say anything?" So I did, and what I've come to suggest in this lesson, ladies, is why don't we just do more of the little things and let it go? It can stop a whole lot of the little disagreements. You know what would have happened if I had left his mess and said something? He would have begun to point out everything he ever saw me leave on my side of the sink. I would have denied it and said my sink was clean and pretend it always is.

I am just being honest because I want to help you ladies understand that we have to let these trivial things in marriage go, because these trivial disagreements can blow up into large disagreements, lots of finger pointing, old reminders of what never was, new reminders of what never will be, and then we're screaming and yelling about stuff in the past, stuff that won't happen in the future, and then we're worn out and not speaking. All because he left toiletries on the sink, he wouldn't flush the toilet, he leaves the seat up and you want it down. We argue because of a drawer being left open, and the other refuses to close it without saying something about what they had to do and how they had to go out of their way to do it. The light is off, you want it on. The light is on, you want it off. Why are we arguing over these trivial things? Nobody warned us that marriage would present so many trivial disagreements.

I remember at one point in my marriage years ago, I got sick and tired of my husband telling me he was always the one who had to replace the toilet paper on the holder and that I never took the time to do it. I knew this was false, so I began storing and saving the empty rolls each time I replaced the roll, so I could prove to him that he was wrong. I wore myself out collecting cardboard rolls and, in the meantime, to teach me a lesson of pettiness, God has made sure he has never said it again, so I finally had to give up and throw them all away.

My point in this lesson is to make you understand that you cannot continue to wear your spouse out, wear yourselves out and, most of all, wear your marriage out over the trivial things, because big matters, big problems are coming and if you are worn out and your marriage is torn down over the little stuff, you are not going to have any strength or be able to find any reason to fight to stay together when the big stuff comes; you will simply be too tired, just too tired. And we have to recognize how the enemy plans to destroy your marriage.

I say it all the time in every class I teach and every chapter I write in my books: the enemy desires to destroy your husband, your children, and you. He wants to tear your marriage apart, his sole desire is to wear you out. The bad part is that we let him. Why? Because we don't know enough about God's Word, and when we don't have enough knowledge of God's Word, we fail to recognize when he is attempting to launch or has already launched an attack against us. Usually when we realize what has happened, it's too late, because we have already gone two or three days without speaking, and that is simply too long. If you are angry that long—I said it before—the spirit of Jesus Christ does not control you. Jesus is love, He has a heart of love and a spirit to love and forgive. Better than that, his greatest command to us is to love, and if you don't believe me, read the scripture text that follows.

> *For God so loved the world that He gave us his only*
> *begotten son. So that whosoever believed would not*
> *parish but have everlasting life.*
> *(John 3:16)*

This means that whoever says that they believe in Jesus Christ should have a spirit a love and a heart to forgive swiftly. I suggest a heart that is unable to forgive or a heart unable to love is not a heart that belongs to Jesus Christ. I don't care how you pray, how you praise, how you treat your children, if you cannot forgive your husband swiftly and move on, you don't have the heart of Jesus Christ.

Okay! So here it comes. "Adrienne, you don't understand." I'm afraid I do. It was one of the hardest lessons I ever learned. And God, not Adrienne, requires me to teach to you not just the things that I have heard about, but things I have personally experienced and gone through; so, yes, I say it again and again, I understand. Yes, I hear you saying, "This man calls me names." Forgive him, you've called other people names before. You've called him names before. "This man cheated on me." Forgive him, you cheated on God before. "This man whips and disciplines my children." It's a command of God. Get over it. God whips and disciplines you. He's whipping some of you right now as you read this chapter.

Ladies, do you know what will keep you out of heaven more than anything else? Do you know what God's greatest command to Jesus was while He walked this earth? Do you know what Jesus' greatest command was to us before He ascended to heaven? "Love each other." Do you know that Jesus could have saved himself at any time before He was crucified? But He knew He was here, assigned by God, to fulfill a promise to his father to save us so that we might be free. He loved us so much that He trusted God and did so to his death. He died so that we could have life more abundantly and we don't know how to receive the abundance, we don't know how to live so that God may be pleased with us and receive the glory, because we have a fight in us, a war in us that we keep trying to control and that we cannot control without the Holy Power of God, but we won't give it to Him. We won't trust that He sees everything that is happening to us in our marriages. So we just keep getting in the way. Every time we near a breakthrough, we get in the way. We do something, we say something. Women, we talk too much. We nag too much. You know why I don't allow women to talk about their husbands in the classes I teach? We talk too much. We're like Energizer bunnies, we keep going and going. What good does all the talking do? None, it does no good. Here you have stayed on the phone with your girlfriend, your co-worker, your mama, your aunt, your sister, your sister in law, three or four hours, all night long, just bashing the poor man. Listening to bad advice, and he still not home, he still didn't quit drinking, he is still over at Delilah's, he is still mad as hell.

Did it ever cross your mind that maybe his problem is you? You won't give him a break. "You need to be home early." "You need to help me around the house more." "You need to fix my car." "You need to go to church more." "You need to come to counseling with me."

"You need to spend more time with the kids." "You need to help me cook." "You need to help me wash clothes." Wife, helpmate, support system, you need to be quiet and give the man a break. You're wearing him out. You're wearing him down. His day has been bad enough. He's been fighting his boss, the traffic, Earl, Ray and Joe. He doesn't need to come home and fight you too. That could be why he is laying his head in Delilah's lap now. You think he doesn't know you're on the phone for hours bashing him with your friends, your family and co-workers? He knows. Wives, men are not really dumb and crazy, they just act that way to keep from dealing with a nagging wife. They pretend they didn't hear you, they pretend they didn't know. It's a defense system; they secretly hope that if they tell us they didn't hear us or they didn't know, we will leave them alone about it.

Ladies, stop nagging him over the little stuff. Pray for Godly wisdom, Godly direction and guidance. God will tell you what to say, when to say it and how to say it. God is the only one who can really save your marriage, and He knew wives would nag. He knew we would have a tendency to want to rule the husband, because we came from the husband. So we are physically and spiritually a part of the husband. So we know what the husband really needs to be doing, but we cannot force him to do it and all the nagging in the world will not make him do what we want. It drives them away from us. I have scripture. It's found in the New Living Translation:

It is better to live in the corner of the attic (the roof)
than with a contentious woman in a lovely home.
(Proverbs 25: 24)

He did not retaliate when He was insulted. When He
suffered, He did not threaten to get even. He left his
case in the hands of God who always judges fairly.
(I Peter 2:23)

Never pay back evil for evil to anyone. Do things in
such a way that everyone can see you are honorable.
(Romans 12:17)

A gentle answer turns away wrath, but harsh words
stir up anger.
(Proverbs 15:1)

Wives, I say this not to hurt anyone, but only to help you understand why your marriages are hard. There is too much nagging and not enough prayer. There is not enough submission to God's word. There is not enough submission to your husbands. There is no peace in your home, so he leaves. If he doesn't leave, he's afraid to talk to you because you begin to whine and complain instead of taking your moans and grumblings to God. There are too many spirits of retaliation in your marriage. There's too much evil for evil. There are too many harsh words and strife. And I am sorry to tell you, because I know I am talking to a group of liberated, strong and educated women, but your are all going to have to calm down, sit down and get in the place that God put you in when He formed you. That place is beside your husband. You may be a leader at work, you may be large and in charge at church, or in your various tasks and assignments, but in marriage you are a helpmate, a support system, and you are called to humbleness, you are called to meekness, quietness, gentleness, forgiveness and love.

So take your business suit off, come home and put your wife clothes on, your helper clothes on, your peace clothes on, your strength clothes on, your submission and respect clothes on and be a wife, his wife the wife God called you to be. We have to stop yelling at these men and destroying their spirits. We have to stop embarrassing them in public and attacking their egos.

Study your Bibles, ladies. Read the Old Testament. Men were built for war, to fight the enemy to defeat the enemy, to keep his family from harm and to head his house. We have become so liberated in these times that the war is in the man's own house, the enemy has slipped into your spirit so your man gets more peace away from home than while in the home. So we have actually helped Satan reverse God's Plan. Instead of the man of God, the warrior protecting the home from the enemy on the outside and coming home to peace, the man is actually finding more peace outside of the home. We have to get it together, wives, and we can't do this alone. We have to reverse the curse, take down and destroy the stronghold that Satan has planted in our minds and our marriages. Stop looking at him and saying, "I really believe if he would change the way he thinks and does things, our marriage would be better." You change. You change the way you think and do things. You change the way you act and I guarantee he'll change the way he acts. Be kinder, even when you feel he has done you wrong. Be kinder, forgive more.

I hear you saying, "Adrienne, you are really asking a lot." Look, I did it. At the worst times of my marriage I did it, and the truth be told, I did it well. God was pleased with me. I know He was, because I was pleased with myself. "How can I become more kind?" you ask. "How can I pull down strongholds?" "How can I break this curse on marriages in my family line?" Come into full obedience of God's word. Study the word of God; fast, tithe, study, and pray. I can only promise you this: you can keep trying everything else, but only God's Word is true. Nothing else will work and nothing else will save your marriage. Nothing else will heal the pains and heartaches that exist from so many mistakes you have made in the past.

You will have to ask God to show you yourself. You will have to begin praying a sincere prayer that He show you the things that you need to change about you in this marital relationship. And be ready to deal spiritually with the things He shows you about yourself. Don't try to fight, push it away or say it was not the Holy Spirit. The Holy Spirit is truth; it will not lie. Once you ask Him to reveal to you yourself, He will.

Maybe you're too weak in some areas, maybe you're top strong, maybe you're too forceful or not forceful enough in other areas where you should be. But most of all, maybe you're not showing enough love, Godly love, Agape love, forgiving love.

Love is patient and kind
(I Corinthians 13: 4)

You ask "How do I get this kind of love?" "How can I become that way?" It is only by giving the Holy Spirit permission to have life in you. It is only by telling Jesus Christ that his spirit can overtake you. It is only by praying that the Holy Spirit live completely in you. Finally I say to you this scripture:

> *But when the Holy Spirit controls our lives, He will produce this kind of fruit in us; love, joy, peace, patience, kindness, goodness, faithfulness, gentleness and self-control. Against such things there is no law.*
> *(Galatians 5: 22, 23a)*

Wives, the word says if your brother is caught in sin, you who are spiritual should restore him gently. Now if you are *not* spiritual, you will not be able to do this, because the passage of scripture this comes from, found in Galatians 6: 1, goes on to warn you that you must restore him carefully, because if you don't you may also be tempted. Verse 2 of this text says, "Carry each other's burdens, and in this way you will fulfill the law of Christ."

Wives, I plead with you that if you want your marriages blessed, that you learn and strive to obey the laws of God. Be loving, be kind, be strong in your wisdom and knowledge. Carry your husband's burdens and fulfill the law of Christ.

A Special Prayer for a Wife

Lord, I come humbly before you right now with a
spirit of submission on behalf of every wife
everywhere listening to sound of my voice or
reading this text. I pray right now, Father, that
you would touch their hearts and minds. I pray
that you would allow them to grant you
permission to take over their spirits right now,
that they would give you permission to not only
just live inside of them but to have life, to take
control of their spirits so they can love their
mates as you called them to do. I pray they would
begin to use wisdom before they speak, and they
would seek a spirit of gentleness before they
correct or offer opinion. Lord, be present now as
I pray. In Jesus' Name, Amen.

*The Lord still waits for you to come to Him so He can
show you his love and compassion. For the Lord is a
faithful God. Blessed are those who wait for Him.
(Isaiah 30:18)*

He Won't Flush the Toilet
Worksheet for Small Groups

Topics to discuss:

What has God spoken to you during this chapter that you hear Him telling you to change?

What irritated your flesh most about this chapter?

What did God tell you to change immediately?

What does the word "meekness" mean to you?

Talk to your group individually, and explain to them one area in your marriage that you have not shown meekness.

Talk about an area where you can submit or give in more to your husband's desire.

What petty issue have you and your husband become angry about lately?

What could you have done to diffuse this argument, though you refused to bend?

Find negative words for this acronym which can tear down a marriage: P E T T Y

Find positive words for this acronym which can build up a marriage: D I F F U S E

My Solution for this Marriage

I have a call to teach God's people, especially wives, how to stand on faith, put God first, trust Him and believe that He can, until He does. Please hear me, I said I have a call to teach wives to stand on faith, put God first, trust Him and believe that He can, until He does.

You see as I say over and over again, God's plan and desire is for a man and woman to get married, become one flesh, start a family and a generation of people. Let me give you scripture on that. These scriptures in Genesis chapter 1 talk about the beginning.

So God created man in his own image, in the image of God, He created him; male and female He created them. God blessed them and said to them, "Be fruitful and increase in number; fill the earth and subdue it.
(Genesis 1: 27)

That was God's plan. Satan's plan is to attack and weaken the support system, the wife, trick the head of the family, the husband, and shame the house, thus destroying the marriage, the children and the family. Satan recognizes this will anger God. Let me talk to you a minute about Adam and Eve. We all know Adam and Eve right? Adam and Eve was the first married couple talked about in the Bible, and they started out very blessed. They were the first ecologists, which means they were the first to name animals. They were the first to tend a garden, the first to be placed in charge of the creatures, the first to have a relationship with God, but also the first to sin.

In Genesis 3:3 it verifies that God said to them, "You must not eat fruit from the tree that is the middle of the garden, and you must not touch it or you will die." God had given them a paradise. He gave them everything they could have wanted, but a nagging thought made them think they were missing something. Has God ever blessed you, and you knew it was a blessing from God, but you allowed a nagging thought make you think of ways the blessing could have been better? With the nagging thought, the enemy was able to make humans think they were missing something in life and become disobedient to the strict word of a loving God.

Adam and Eve were tricked by the enemy into thinking God was holding back on something. So they ate from the forbidden tree; you see right from the beginning, human beings disobeyed God and we have been suffering for that disobedience every since. God's original plan for us was to live in Paradise, in a life of luxury, not working or having pain, but just living a relaxed and simple life. The instruction was just obey all that He had commanded of them, and at that time, the only command was to not eat from the tree in the middle of the garden.

I could teach on the beginning for a quite a while, but that is not what this chapter is about. I just wanted you to understand that it's only because of our sin and disobedience that we have to labor so hard and suffer so much pain, and please don't take that lightly. In your spare time, read Genesis chapter 3 so you can obtain a full understanding of why we labor and suffer in childbirth; it is the curse that God placed on us for disobedience to his command. Can you imagine how Adam and Eve must have argued when God became angry and asked them why they ate from the forbidden tree? Eve blaming Adam for being the head and not putting his foot down and Adam blaming Eve for presenting the temptation to him. Eve probably said, "You ate the fruit." Adam speaking back, "You gave it to me." Anyway, in the end, they were banished from Paradise. You know another thing this caused. God's original plan was for the woman to be beside the man in all matters, but because of this sin, God said, "No more. No longer will you be beside the man, He will rule over you." That is in verse 16. He said, "Your desire will be for the husband to rule over you, because of this sin." This verse explains why the wife is supposed to accept the authority of her husband for a successful marriage.

Could this be why we struggle in our marriages? We were originally designed to be beside our husbands, but because of sin, God commands us to want them to rule over us. That's deep and a whole different lesson.

My point is that because of sin and disobedience, we struggle and suffer pain in our marriages. This that I speak about is Old Testament and in the Old Testament, we were under God's law. In the New Testament, we have a Risen Savior named Jesus Christ. Because Jesus came to save us, we are no longer under the law, but we are now under grace.

This does not discount the Old Testament. The Old Testament merely just means God's law was the final word, and I thank God for Jesus every day. Because under God's law, you will find that when a person sinned and disobeyed God's law or his command, He destroyed you. He killed you, right there on the spot. There was no time to explain or beg for forgiveness from Christ because He was not yet born.

Like my Pastor would say, "Come here, Lot's wife." Yes, when they were being rescued from Sodom, the word tells us that God commanded for Lot and his family to leave Sodom swiftly and not look back... and Lot's wife turned to see what was going on after the command of God said, "Run for your life, and don't look back," and she died.

When God realized, after destroying and rebuilding the earth, that we just had evil hearts and were going to be sinners, He said, "These people need a Savior. They need someone to cover their sins." So He sent us Jesus, his only begotten son, so that we would not die, but have everlasting life. Again, that's a whole different chapter.

The point is, now we are married. We have Jesus, and we still are suffering in our marriages. Why? Because of disobedience and sin. There are rules/commands in marriage. Commands for the husband, and commands for the wife and we are not following those commands and we continue, like Adam and Eve, to blame one another. There is too much "he says, she says" in marriage, there is too much "tit for tat," and someone has to be the bigger person and say, "no more." Someone has to say, "I am going to die to this flesh, live for Christ and say no to the devil."

"What do you mean, Adrienne? Say 'no' to the devil?" You see, God blessed marriages from the beginning as I said earlier, and Satan is still deceiving husbands, and Satan is still deceiving wives, so much so that this year you have decided to leave. "No more!" you have said. "You have hurt me too long, you have kept us struggling to long, you have held me back too long." No he didn't. You have done those things to yourself, because you won't let God's hand rule you and guide you. You won't become a virtuous wife as described in Proverbs 31: 10-31. You won't become meek in your spirit and kind in your words. "Adrienne, he won't stop drinking." I know, but you won't stop cursing him out about it. "Adrienne, he won't stop spending all the money." I know, but you won't stop trying to handle the situation alone without God. "Adrienne, he won't stop coming home at 5:00 in the morning or staying out all night." I know, but you won't go to sleep and trust God.

Let's talk about you. You won't stop coming to church and going home, slinging the Bible all in his face. You won't stop nagging him about his habit that only prayer can change. You won't stop giving in to the enemy's attacks. His spirit attacks you and you lay your religion down and attack back. You know what? I have heard so many people say, "I had to lay my religion down and get him told…." My question is: how do you lay something down that lives inside of you? How do you lay down the Spirit of Christ? How do you lay Jesus down to curse someone out?

If you can simply take the Holy Spirit that lives inside of you and lay it down while you get someone told, pick it back up, put it back inside of you, and say you are a child of God, then apparently I am missing something. That is truly a miracle I have yet to see.

So because of the disobedience in your marriage, you have made a good clear decision that this is the year it's over. God has said it, it's final, and that's my New Year's resolution. You have talked to your friends and family, they have given you the go ahead and said, "That's good, good decision." "Leave that drunk, leave that drug addict, leave that gambler, leave that curser, that fool, that abuser, that lawbreaker, leave him, that's good, you have finally come to your senses."

My question is, "Have you really finally come to your senses?" What are the 5 senses? Sight, Smell, Hear, Feel, and Taste.

Who gave us these senses? God, so to say you have come to your senses means you have come to the full realization of God. So, if you have come to this full realization in your marriage and you have decided to leave your marriage because you have heard from God, my assignment is to help you make sure so you can continue in your good and right decision.

First, let's make sure you have truly heard from God by going over these scriptures. Now I don't want to stop you from leaving because your decision has been made, and your conscious is clear, but my call as a Preacher, a Prophetess, a Teacher a Minister of God's word, is to help you come to the full realization of Jesus Christ, God and His word.

> *And unto the married I command yet not I but the Lord, Let not the wife depart from her husband: But and if she departs let her remain unmarried or be reconciled to her husband: and let not the husband put away his wife.*
> *(I Corinthians 7:10 -11)*

This is the only scripture in the Bible that I could find that justifies a wife separating from her husband. Keep in mind, it reminds the wife that if she separates she must remain unmarried. There is no provision for sleeping with another man because you are separated. Know that I do understand divorce happens, but as we continue in this book, I will help you, wife, understand that this provision for divorce speaks to the man.

Wife, I have studied the scriptures and in all situations just as Job went through even in disaster and terror, God's word says be strong and courageous, trust me and I will see you through. So keep in mind, even if you separate from your husband and this will generally happen in abusive situations, drug and alcohol use or other excessive behaviors, you are called to pray for healing and reconciliation. But the scripture is very general as it states, "Let not the wife depart from her husband." Women stop leaving your homes in the midst of rocky trials which only threaten to shatter the marriage; it does not have to happen. You have a God who has all power to change all circumstances.

> *The wife is bound by the law as long as her husband*
> *liveth, but if her husband be dead, she is at liberty to*
> *be married to whom she will: only in the Lord.*
> *(I Corinthians 7:39)*

This is a powerful scripture that discusses God's command to a wife. This is why many more couples need to seek premarital counseling before marriage, because we go into marriage too lightly without a clear understanding of what the Lord commands regarding marriage. This text tells us that the wife is married to this husband as long as he is alive. This means that only after his death are you free to marry another. The second husband must be approved by God.

> *And the woman which hath an husband that believeth*
> *not, and he be pleased to dwell with her, let her not*
> *leave him. But if the unbelieving depart, let him*
> *depart. A brother or sister is not under bondage in*
> *such cases; but God has called us to peace.*
> *(I Corinthians 7: 13, 15)*

I love teaching this passage of scripture in the wives' classes I teach, because I can have so much fun with it. You see, many wives would prefer that their unbelieving spouses who never go to church with them or only go on the two church holidays (Christmas and Easter) would really prefer their husbands be gone from them, but this scripture tells us that even if you are Holy Ghost filled, saved, baptized with fire, sanctified, and stay in church seven days a week and your unsaved husband is in love with you and pleased to have you as his wife, then you are not to leave him. How is that for a command from God? I love it.

Now if, and only if, the husband leaves you, are you freed from this marriage. I tell all the wives in my classes, "Don't go and try to make your husband leave you. But if your husband leaves you, you are not under bondage." God has called you to peace. Let me repeat that, God has called you to peace. So if you come home and he has left; God has called you to peace. Why are you stalking him? Why are you chasing him down and trying to run him over at his workplace? Why are you showing up at his apartment or home breaking windows and breaking in? He left you. God has called you to peace. If you want him back, go home and pray. He is your husband. You have the power of God and the favor of God. You are the wife. However all of this sin and disobedience against God's word will *not* give you favor with God or with him.

Genesis 2:24 says you are one flesh anyway, so he is with you always anyway. Allow your husband to go through this wilderness experience, worldly known as a midlife crisis, he doesn't even love himself; how can you expect him to love you? At these times when Satan has attacked his spirit and is seeking to kill him and remove him from the one who has been carrying him through in prayers, is the time you must be the helpmate and pray daily for a covering of blood protection over him. Believe me when I say this. When our men are under this type of attack and they have left the home for no good reason, then this is the time a wife must pray. You must not nag, you must not beg them to come home, you must not yell, scream, shout and curse. You must pray.

Now if you have committed adultery and your husband knows about it, then under God's law, you have no rights as a wife. You have no favor. I have had wives sit in my office and tell me that they have cheated and their husband has now cheated and left and they wonder why they can't get him back, don't ask me. Ask God. God's word is what it is, and He built men in his image. I guess God does not like a woman cheating on him. I personally and scripturally suggest that a woman, once she is married no matter what the circumstances, should not be laying down and spreading herself for another man, especially if she plans to stay married. Again, this is why we have to begin making sure as Pastors, ministers and counselors that couples begin to have premarital counseling. This word is final. Sound unfair? Let's go to the next scripture.

> *Since they are no longer two but one, let no one*
> *separate them, for God has joined them together.*
> *Then why did Moses say a man could merely write*
> *and official letter of divorce and send her away?*
> *They asked. Jesus replied, "Moses permitted divorce*
> *as a concession to your hardhearted wickedness, but*
> *it was not what God originally intended. And I tell*
> *you this, a man who divorces his wife and marries*
> *another commits adultery-unless the wife has been*
> *unfaithful." [11] Not everyone can accept this statement*
> *Jesus said. "Only those whom God helps."*
> *(Matthew 19: 6-9, 11)*

This scripture passage is clear, it tells us that the two has become one, and no one should separate them. God hates divorce, his plan is for families and down through the line families. Divorce was placed in the Bible only as a provision to forgive us for our hard heartedness. God knew we would struggle with forgiving others and He knew many of us would want to leave our marriages, so this provision just allows us to be forgiven; it is not God' way or His will.

Now let me explain the scripture: This scripture clearly states to a man, not a woman, that if you divorce your wife, it should only be because she has committed adultery. It does not say a wife can divorce her cheating husband; it clearly states in every version I have read that the man can divorce his wife who has been unfaithful. It follows by saying everyone cannot accept this. Can you? Ask God to help you, I cannot. I can only teach what is the word of God and this is the word of God.

Ladies, I couldn't find a scripture to free you from the law. Finally I ask you to ask yourself, in the scriptures I have shown you and discussed with you, do you still feel you have heard from God? Do you still feel you have come to your senses? Yes, your family is pleased with your decision, your friends are pleased with your decision, but is God pleased with your decision?

This marriage is rough and it is hurting you. You say, "I don't know what God expects of me. I never knew it was this hard. How do I stand by this man?" Let me first say to you: I don't preach divorce and I don't teach divorce, because I can't find anywhere in the Bible where God gives a wife a provision for it except in death.

The provision given in Matthew chapter 19 is for the man. Why? I don't know, you will have to wait and ask God. I know some of you wives reading this book right now are separated from your husbands, but are you in God's will, are you sure of your decision? It is because of faith you bought and are reading this book; it is because you trust God.

I understand that when there is distrust and constant disappointments that your peace is destroyed. Separation is important, and there is a clause for it in I Corinthians 7:10-11, but I beg of you, even in separation, never give up on God, never become disobedient to God's word, by giving up on your spouse. It clearly states, "Let her remain unmarried or be reconciled to her husband." This means while you are apart, you must pray. The reason for separation is totally useless if you leave and you still allow him every opportunity to come over and attack you with useless words and actions. Don't use it as a time to date other men. This is not what it's for. Don't use it as a time to enjoy your freedom in living apart from allowing him, and sleeping with other men and then allowing him every opportunity to come over to sleep with you in between those times. This time to be apart is so that you both may reflect with God and allow God's will to be done in your lives and in your marriage.

During this time, you are to never take your prayers off of him, because even while you are apart, you must always believe that God is able. When there is abuse on your part or his in the marriage, separation is not only good, it is necessary. But just like drinking, gambling, drugs and alcohol; abusiveness is an outward expression which has a underlying cause and it needs prayer, care and counseling. This is the part of the vow that stated, "In sickness and in health." We tend to forget that part of our commitment when the road gets rough and rocky.

A generational cause, a genetic curse. These sins in marriage are normally due to underlying causes that families have never discussed and have always been ashamed to talk about openly or with anyone. So as wives to these husbands who suffer and become attacked genetically with these spirits planted by the enemy, we are never told.

Because his grandmother or his mother won't tell you his grandfather was an abuser or a drug addict or an alcoholic, they won't tell you. In fact, they will say things like, "I don't know why he's like that. He just crazy like his daddy was, I guess."

And it's time for honesty in these families so these curses and evil spirits passed down genetically can be broken. Most men who exhibit these characteristics have a pain on the inside so deep that comes from a past issue that only God can fix. You can't fix it because you don't know how deep it goes. You can't fix it, because you are not God. And when that spirit of damnation is on the inside of that husband, or even you the wife in some cases, only a touch from God, only by a plea of the blood, only by supplication which is a specific prayer request, only by the laying of anointed hands can this demonic spirit be called out. And men who are unhappy with themselves, men who anger easily, men who drink, gamble, smoke, and commit adultery excessively, have a pain on the inside that a wife cannot comfort or cure. Only God!

Wives, stop beating yourselves up trying to please this pain in your husband, stop stressing and losing yourselves by coming entwined in a war with Satan and turn this man over to God. Move back, step back and pray for him. Wives, you have the power of God to stand, to stay and to call out those spirits. You have the Holy Power of God living inside of you to change things in your home, to change rulership; but you must submit your will to God.

Satan does not have to rule your home… and the truth be told, that's why you decided to leave; that is why you have decided to run. You are tired of fighting the enemy who controls your spouse.

Ladies, the good news is you don't have to run and you don't have to fight the enemy. Turn it over to Jesus. Become the Proverbs women in chapter 31. Stop trying to preach to the spirit of the enemy. He can't hear you. It's not your husband you fight. You see his face, but it is the enemy that controls him that you fight, and you are trying to fight him without God's power. I know you say right now, "I have Jesus, I fight with Jesus." No ,you don't. Jesus doesn't fight with skillets, knives, curse words, guns, and hatred. Jesus fights with Forgiveness and Love.... That is how Jesus fights.... It's the hardest lesson, but it is the greatest lesson.

I will close this chapter by quoting from the NIV. The book of Corinthians was written by Paul and I find Paul to be the greatest teacher on suffering and persecution because of his trust in God. I want to be like Paul, and I want you to become like Paul as wives.... Only then will you come to your senses. The scripture reads:

We are fools for Christ! We are weak, but you are strong!
You are honored, we are dishonored! To this very hour we
go hungry and thirsty, we are in rags, we are brutally
treated, we are homeless. We work hard with our own
hands. When we are cursed, we bless; when we are
persecuted we endure it; when we are slandered, we
answer kindly. Up to this moment we have become the
scum of the earth, the refuge of the world.
(I Corinthians 4: 10-14)

The text goes on to say that he is not writing to shame you, but to warn you as children of God, you must endure and remain faithful unto Christ. Don't become arrogant, the Kingdom of God is not a matter of talk but of power.

I struggle in my marriage, just as you do. I fight the enemy, just as you do. My home is attacked by Satan, just like yours. I said before, Satan has no favorites, he wants to wear all marriages out. The difference is I have learned by faith to overcome the enemy through our Lord and Savior Jesus Christ, and I pray now that you will receive that same victory in your life.

Delilah Doesn't Have to Ruin Your Marriage

*Or else, how can one enter into a strongman's house
and spoil his goods, except he first bind the
strongman? And then he will spoil his house.
(Matthew 12:29)*

This chapter will focus on and give us a clear understanding of the different types of attacks that will come against our marriages. This chapter will show us that Satan's priority is to invade, sabotage, divide, cause separation and eventually destroy our homes.

God's plan was that men and women would get married and not only have, but raise together, sons and daughters. Unfortunately, because of a lack of knowledge and understanding as it relates to God's word, in many cases God's plan for marriage is not carried out.

My ministry that you will often hear me speak of throughout this book, Holy Matrimony Prophetic Ministries, was organized not for married women who have problems in their marriage as some are lead to believe, this ministry was organized because we as wives need support and encouragement even in a good marriage. We need a clear understanding of the warfare that attacks our homes and we need to know how God's power can help us defeat those attacks. In many cases, Satan's attack is so swift and abrupt that it literally wipes us off of our feet. At those times, instead of immediately jumping to conclusions and playing the blame game, we need to understand scripturally what has happened. We need to understand that it is warfare that has invaded our homes and it is designed by Satan to threaten, to destroy God's plan for the family and the marriage. Because *so many of us don't understand,* Satan is winning.

Marriages are breaking up like never before. The average marriage is barely making it to seven years, and those who make it to that point have struggled to get that far. Many that even make it to the seven-year mark are not healthy and are sitting on the edge of a dangerous cliff. This means that with one sudden tremble, one sudden shake, the marriage will begin sliding downhill and will never gain its balance, because it is not in God's will or God's plan.

So what question should we be asking of God? I say: "Lord, show me how recognize the Stronghold that has attacked my home." But do you know what is so unfortunate in asking that question? This is not to put anyone down, but unfortunately in some marriages, it is because we have been so far away from God's will and His plan. There are so many strongholds in the home, the battle seems overwhelming, and you feel as though you are fighting a lose, lose situation. But that is not to say God can't help, because He can fix any situation.

The question is, "How do I recognize when a stronghold has attacked my home?" The answer is by praying to God for your ability through the Holy Spirit to discern the strongholds in your life. You see, we must recognize what it is we should be praying for and, like King Solomon prayed, we must also first be praying for wisdom and knowledge. Because until we understand how God reveals the attacks of the enemy, we will not be able to stand, and we will not be able to fight, and we will walk around most of our marriage feeling literally worn out with no joy in our hearts or laughter in our spirits. I promise you, however, that once you begin to recognize the enemy, you will not cry as much or worry as often. You will soon be able to laugh at him and go about your day.

The next question: "Once God allows me to identify a stronghold, am I strong enough to fight against it?" The answer is No! Definitely not, you are not strong enough to fight against any attack that comes against your marriage, but the Holy Spirit Power of God that lives within you is strong enough and will fight on your behalf. You see, that is the problem with many of the wives and husbands in marriages represented in the world: you have been trying to fight and stand in your own power, and you cannot. As a matter of fact, for many of you, that is why your matters in your marriage become worse, because you never went to God to ask Him "how" before you made your move. You just thought about your situation, prayed in flesh, said "In Jesus' Name" and stepped out in what you wanted to do, handling it the way you best saw fit and the Holy Spirit had nothing to do with the decision chosen. Yes, many of you made your move, and then you went to God and asked for forgiveness, and God, being the God that He is, forgave you, but the damage was done. The tongues of hellfire had already set the house ablaze and parts of the marriage were burned down, and what was not burned down was singed.

So now you sit and you try to figure a way to restore and it never crosses your mind you still need Jesus Christ. Only Jesus Christ, the Son of God, can fix a Holy Institution ordained by his Father, our God.

For the weapons of war are not carnal, but mighty
through God to the pulling down of strongholds.
(2 Corinthians 10:4)

This scripture clearly states to us that we cannot fight with carnal or fleshly weapons. Our weapons are only mighty through God.

That is why premarital counseling is so important, because it teaches us how to communicate effectively with one another. It gives us the opportunity to advance, to discuss with one another children, finances, housekeeping, employment, and other expectations we will have of each other, and then this stuff which tears down so many marriages is not able to fester and take us by surprise.

Question: Can God help even in my situation? My husband and I have almost declared our situation as hopeless.

Answer: Yes. God can.

*For this purpose, the Son of God was manifested that
He might destroy the works of the devil.
(I John 3:8)*

Let's get into some of the weapons that Satan will use to come against your marriage. These weapons are called strongholds. I know by now you are saying, "Well, Adrienne, I thought this chapter was entitled, 'Delilah Does Not Have to Ruin Your Marriage.'" It is, and she does not have to ruin your marriage. You see, Delilah is simply a stronghold, and in the story of Samson and Delilah, the Bible only shows us how a woman was used as a form of seduction to destroy a man and his marriage. But another woman is not the only form of destruction a stronghold comes in, and that is why I always teach wives to stop letting another woman or an affair dictate that your marriage is over.

Satan has many weapons he will use to attack your home, unfortunately because of the useful lust and foolish hearts of men and some women, adultery is one of his most powerful and common weapons he uses to tear down the union. Because adultery attacks the heart, it can literally destroy the mind of a committed spouse. That is why in marriage, your heart has to be totally committed to God, because a heart committed to a spouse in the case of adultery and many other strongholds is a heart that will cause the mind to become weak. Now I am *not* saying that when you are saved and your heart is completely submitted to God, these attacks won't hurt. Many of them still will hurt very much. What I am saying is when your heart is completely submitted to Christ and this type of attack comes, your flesh won't be able to easily take over because the Holy Spirit which controls you will only allow you to fight with God's power and His word. The word of God is all you need to get through these storms.

*Jesus replied, "Love the Lord your God with all your
heart and with all your soul and with all your mind."
(Matthew 22: 37)*

CINDERELLA, YOU LIED TO ME.

I come to suggest that too many of us have not given God our hearts, minds, and souls, but we have given those to our spouses. This is why we hurt and get offended so easily, because too much of what God told us to give Him has been given to men.

My point in all of this is that even when we are not really feeling the love anyway that we are supposed to be feeling for our spouses, an affair somehow indicates betrayal and causes us to seek vengeance.

Pride is also a stronghold in a marriage, and even if the love is gone and we're just hanging onto a thread of commitment, when adultery comes to a marriage, most of our anger is not so much because what we have found out has hurt us; it is our pride that has been hurt, because we thought our circumstances were above such an attack.

We never stop to look or ask God how the enemy was able to sneak into our marriages and slip in such an attack, yet our pride and selfishness usually comes in full force and begin saying , "I can't believe he did this to me, he must not know who I am," and all sorts of such foolish talk. We never stop to look at ourselves and try to figure out what role we played, how many harmful words we said, how many nights did we not cook, or how many nights did we withheld sex and slashed his character with our tongue.

Do you want me to tell you the biggest mistake many new wives make? The big one! You bring too many single Delilahs into your homes to spend days alone with you and your spouse. Yeah, I know he is your man, he is different, he is strong, and your friend would never seduce your husband. No, she wouldn't, but Satan would. Just think on that. Wives, Satan is a temptor and the male is weak. Don't assist Delilah in her task. I don't care how much you love her. Sound weak? Maybe you're saying, "I am secure in my marriage; that advice is not for me." No, that advice is for every married woman, even you, the one who feels very secure in the marriage. Satan has no favorites, except for those he can send your way to do the best job at destroying your relationship with your husband. Have you ever had a single friend come over and ask you right in front of your husband, "Why you don't clean and cook more?" That's a good friend. How about this one? "Do you like your wife's hair like that?" How about this one?

47

"You should do your dishes more." "No I am just teasing." Does it seem like she just knew all the sticklers between you and your husband? No, she just knew what the problems were in the last relationship she was in and decided to try them out in your marriage. But that is your girlfriend, so you will move past those things. After all, you're secure in your marriage. What's the harm of a few little jabs from a friend?

Then we move too many people into our homes with us and they stay too long. We never stop to wonder how we moved in or permitted him to move in all these family members.... God's word says a man will leave his father and mother and cling unto his wife.... We have to stop thinking we can move in our aunts, uncles, brothers, long-lost cousins, nieces and nephews and they will not interfere in God's plan for marriage. The word of God does not stutter.

I have even talked to wives who allow female friends and old female friends from high school to just call and chat with their husband. How long, wife, do you think that will last before Satan starts letting this friend have more influence in his life and in his decisions than you do? Wives, we have to be wise and pray for a spirit of discernment and wisdom in all matters of marriage. We're fighting hard and losing the game, because we are trying to take an institution that God ordained as Holy and live it according to the world's standards.

Let me make this plain, because some of you women are throwing what I just said into the trash as though your marriage is above it. I said *no women should be calling your home to have small talk and chit chat with your husband.* It ruins men and marriages. Some things in marriage you just don't tolerate. This is one area. Unless it is a business call or a conversation relating to work or business, it should not be made or get through. He hasn't even learned how to spend quality time with you and your own kids. Why is he on the phone talking to and old friend about her problems and her kids? Now that's just Adrienne, but it has worked in my now-twenty-seven years of marriage.

Other women should not be dropping by and sitting in your home waiting for you with your husband. It is out of order and a set up by Satan. If she comes by and you are not home, if she doesn't want to wait outside in her car, your man should have sense enough to tell her that she can come back later when you are home. The enemy is tricky and he carefully starts in areas such as these to begin planning his scheme of deception.

Satan carefully plants his seeds, just like God, and when God's seeds are sprouting, so are the ones the enemy planted. You will generally know his have sprouted when all Hell has broken loose in your home and you didn't see it coming. And because you catered more to the ones Satan planted with all this permissiveness in your marriage, God's seeds planted in your marriage never sprout, because they are choked by the weeds of seeds from Satan. Then the next thing you know, he is laying in someone else's arms telling her all about you and what you don't do to please him, sharing stuff with her that you have been trying to get him to share with you for years.

Strongholds!

Strongholds that have slowly invaded your marriage have sprouted their ugly heads. That is why I wish I could help wives understand it is the hand of the enemy they should be fighting against with God's power and not their husbands. Adultery, it is his oldest form of seduction which destroys lives, marriages, children and homes.

And, wives, stop thinking that if your husband gets saved and filled with the Holy Spirit, his mind will never be attacked again and he will become sin free. He will not. David, a man after God's own heart, committed adultery, planned a murder and carried it out, then had a baby outside of his marriage. After which he tried to cast the woman aside. Though forgiven and still greatly loved by God, he was a sinner and God caused him to reap greatly all that evil which he had sown. I suggest in this that God is forgiving, however sin and temptation will fall upon all of us, and we must fight with God's power against all sin, and all strongholds which threaten our homes.

This leads me to the many faces of Delilah. Though I wanted to discuss Delilah as adultery, I want you to understand the many faces of Delilah. We have got to stop thinking she is the most destructive force to come. We must remember she just hurts the most because she is both sexual and emotional. Remember, as I said earlier, she affects the heart.

Take note of the other Delilahs which will threaten your home. Keep in mind, God has all power, and through His power, you have victory in every thing and in every attack; however, these certainly all play a great role at making attempts to tear down your marriage. I will list the most outward first, that almost immediately see and advise our friends to leave their husbands. Yeah, we do, the Great women of Faith that we are, tell our friends to leave their husbands.

Best Known Delilahs

* The Other Woman
* Drug Addiction
* Alcohol
* Gambling
* Anger/Rage
* Verbal/Physical Abuse
* Lack of Employment
* The Unsaved Spouse
* Lying and Deceit
* Manipulation
* Scornfulness
* Hatred
* Contempt
* Self-righteous Attitudes
* Strife/conflict
* Arrogance
* Laziness
* Vengeance

Should I go on? And these are just some of the Delilahs in your home that, after awhile if you don't pray for a healing over and ask for wisdom and guidance on understanding them, will eventually destroy your marriage.

Earlier I quoted a scripture from Matthew 22:37, in this text it reminds us that we should have no gods, before God, and it stated that we should love only God with our whole heart, mind and soul. Because many of us have made our husbands a god, we cant please God, because we are so busy trying to please our gods, our husbands. In that we are miserable, and we find that no matter what we do, in many cases, we cannot please him. So why not let God be God? You please God by making God first in your life and let God make you pleasing to your husband.

In all your ways, you have tried to please your husband before you have tried to please God, and so finally when you are worn out and exhausted, you ask God, "Why cant I please this man?" God reminds you, "I never told you to, but since you wanted the job and wouldn't let me do it, I released the job to you. Now look at the mess you have made."

So at this point, after fighting God and entertaining strongholds that have beat you up and worn your marriage out, I ask you, "Are you ready to turn all of this over to God, especially the Delilahs that threaten to take this marriage out?"

Wife of Virtue, you have the power through Christ Jesus, but first you must, with a sincere desire and a sincere heart, release your Delilah to him. You have the Holy Spirit Power of God inside of you, who desires to take control of your heart, mind, soul and your present situation. He has been waiting for you to release it all to Him so that He can change your life and your situation.

Like Dorothy in *The Wizard of Oz*, many of you have been in the wilderness, being tricked, being chased by the enemy, and making new friends who are lost as well. Your new friends were all hurt as well and needed many of the same things you needed; one needed a heart, one needed a mind, and one needed courage. There you all were in this strange place trying to make it to this great land where you thought the answers could be found. Only to get there and discover it was all a lie. Because the answer resides within Jesus Christ. Like Dorothy, you put your trust in a man who sent you around and around, seeking only that which God could give you. All the while, God's angels hovered around you and delivered you over and over again, until like Dorothy, you finally realized the answer was in a bucket of water, and always was on the inside of you. The water destroyed the enemy that chased Dorothy, and it can destroy the enemy that deceives you, because it represents purity. The Spirit inside of Dorothy saved her and the Spirit inside of you can save and deliver you, because it represents Christ.

> *Unless a man be born water and Spirit,*
> *he cannot see the Kingdom of God.*
> *(John 3:5)*

God wants to destroy the works of the devil. He wants to save your marriage and He wants you to have all of his power as you defeat Delilah in your marriage.

Lord, I ask that you would bless wives, husbands and marriages right now. I pray a renewed Spirit of Christ in all wives reading this book. In the mighty name of Jesus I pray. Amen.

Standing on the Promise

¹Since you have been raised to new life with Christ, set your sights on the realities of heaven, where Christ sits at God's right hand in the place of honor and power. ² Let heaven fill your thoughts. Do not think only about things down here on earth.
(Colossians 3: 1-2)

⁵So put to death the sinful, earthly things lurking within you. Have nothing to do with sexual sin, impurity, lust, and shameful desires. Don't be greedy for the things of this life, for that is idolatry. ⁶God's terrible anger will come upon those who do such things. ⁷You used to do them when your life was still part of this world. ⁸But now is the time to rid of anger, rage, malicious behavior, slander, and dirty language. ⁹Don't lie to each other, for you have stripped off your old evil nature and all it wicked deeds. ¹⁰In its place you have clothed yourselves with a brand new nature that is continually being renewed as you learn more and more about Christ who created this new nature within you.
(Colossians 3: 5-10)

[12]Since God chose you to be his holy people whom He loves, you must clothe yourselves with tenderhearted mercy, kindness, humility, gentleness, and patience. [13]You must make allowance for each others faults and forgive the person who offends you. Remember the Lord forgave you, so you must forgive others, [14]And the most important piece of clothing you must wear is love. Love is what binds us all together in peace and harmony. [15]And let the peace that comes from Christ rule in your hearts. For as members of one body you are called to live in peace. And always be thankful. [16]Let the words of Christ, in all their richness, live in your hearts and make you wise. Use his words to teach and counsel each other. Sing psalms and hymns and spiritual songs to God with thankful hearts. [17]And whatever you do or say, let it be as a representative of the Lord Jesus, all the while giving thanks through him to God the Father. (Colossians 3: 12-17)

Instructions for Christian Households

[18]You wives must submit to your husbands as is fitting for those who belong to the Lord. [19]Husbands, love your wives and never treat them harshly. [20]You children must always obey your parents, for this is what pleases the Lord. [21]Fathers, don't aggravate your children. If you do, they will become discouraged and quit trying. [25]But if you do what is wrong, you will be paid back for the wrong you have done. For God has no favorites who can get away with evil. (Colossians 3: 18-21, 25)

Write a short paragraph describing what these passages speak to you.

_____

_____

_____

_____

_____

_____

_____

_____

_____

_____

_____

Write a short paragraph describing to God what you immediately realize you need to do better in your marital relationship with your spouse.

_____

_____

_____

_____

_____

_____

_____

_____

_____

_____

_____

You know, in this ministry, I have received so many testimonies from wives and they say to me, "Thank God for Married Women of Virtue. I am a better wife, because I just did not know my spiritual role, my marriage is healing and my husband changing because of my spirit."

Ladies, I thank God for Married Women of Virtue as well, because when I married at the age of nineteen, I didn't know either. But as I let the Lord God's hand lead me through marriage and guide me past my mistakes I never realized that all of the preparation was for a ministry such as this. I didn't realize that my standing, my staying, my crying, my pleading and my praying for a better and stronger marriage would be used some twenty-seven years later for a time and a purpose in the lives of others such as this.

As I teach and put lessons together, I find myself teaching and talking of things that I only usually find in the Bible during my research or after I have taught it, so I know it is God who teaches me all that I teach you.

As I studied and asked God how I am able to teach you what I do, He lead me to this passage of scripture that I must share.

> *But you have received the Holy Spirit and He lives*
> *within you, so you don't need anyone to teach you*
> *what is true. For the Spirit teaches you all things,*
> *and what He teaches you is true; it is not a lie.*
> *So continue in what He has taught you,*
> *and continue to live in Christ.*
> *(I John 2:27)*

When I asked God, "Why me?" He lead me to the book of Titus and confirmed for me in my heart this gift from God.

> *Similarly, teach the older women to live in a way that*
> *is appropriate for someone serving the Lord. They*
> *must not go around speaking evil of others and must*
> *not be heavy drinkers. Instead, they should teach*
> *others what is good. These older women must train*
> *the younger women to love their husbands and their*

*children, to live wisely and be pure, to take care of their
homes, to do good, and to be submissive to their husbands.
Then they will not bring shame on the word of God.
(Titus 2: 3-5)*

Wives, I do not share this so that you may honor me or glorify me, but I share all of this so that you may recognize God's power in your life, even when you are in the midst of circumstances that you now don't understand, that now make no sense. I never understood why I married so young, I never understood so many of the trying circumstances and many different trials and sufferings in my life and in my marriage, but now I do. And I take pleasure and honor in the fact that God chose me to stand and teach, and to write this book to you with a committed and humble heart on how to become a Married Woman of Virtue.

So when I say to you, "Stand through the suffering, and pray," when I say to you, "Never give up on God and the promises and provisions He can make in your circumstances," I speak the truth to you. I speak to you from the many provisions He made for me in my life because of my prayers, even when my husband was not yet seated at the top of the house where he belonged. But I never gave up and I never stopped living a holy life in the sight of God because of His unchanged life.

I prayed, I stood and I waited... and God moved on my behalf. Not in my timing, but in His timing, and I felt I needed to share that with you before we could even move into these scriptures, because if you read this and you don't believe God can or will, then He surely will not. Without faith, it is impossible to please God, and He will not move on your behalf.

*If you need wisdom—if you want to know what God
wants you to do—ask Him, and He will gladly tell
you. He will not resent your asking. But when you ask
Him, be sure that you really expect Him to answer,
for a doubtful mind is unsettled as a wave of the sea
that is driven and tossed by the wind. People like that
should not expect to receive anything from the Lord.
(James 1: 5-7)*

My marriage went through trials and pain shortly after my mother died. My husband was very close to my mother because we married at such a young age, and she accepted him as one of her own sons. He said to me that when my mother died, he felt like he had lost a part of himself because she was an encourager to him, always comforting him and assuring him that he was doing a great job by me and the children; so when she died, my husband also suffered a great loss. At her point of death, Myke began to drink heavily, and from 1994 to 1999 my husband talked about leaving, and Satan used Delilah and every other stronghold he could think of to take him from me and my children. I was alone, my mother had passed away, and my sister stopped speaking to me. All of my brothers' marriages were being attacked by the same curse in their marriages and it seemed Satan began to run rampant in the lives of our family when we lost this pillar. This was how I knew that all the strength I had came from God.

My husband's family had literally terminated their relationship with me, feeling I was the cause of Myke's deteriorating relationship with them. Basically, all Hell was breaking loose in every area of my life, even on my job which happened to be in a church. I was lied to, cheated on, stabbed in the back, and I had absolutely no idea what was going on in my life, but I *never* gave up on God. I never publicly allowed Satan to steal my peace, my joy or my expectation that God would come through for me and work everything out.

When I cried, I cried in secret to the only One who could help me…. I didn't tell any friends what I was going through, and the one family member I attempted to tell advised me that the Bible said in the case of adultery, it was okay for me to divorce my husband. That was not my interpretation or my belief, so I immediately knew it was not the voice of God speaking through him, but it was God telling me to be quiet and let him have it all, and he's telling someone else that same thing, "Be quiet, stop talking, and let me have it all.

For four years, I walked around, bleeding from swords being thrown and knives slicing me, but I had no one but God to talk to or tell. I was very alone, in a place I had never been before and I knew it was God who had placed me there, because I asked Him. Yes, one day I said, "God, why did you have all of this happen to me after my mother has died and I have no one to talk to?" My sister being four years older than me was dealing with my mother's death in her own way, and she really disowned the entire family while she went through her own pain. Understanding it was God doing something greater in her, all of my brothers and I let her have that time. As God began to answer my question, He stated very clearly to me, "I secluded you so that you could only depend on Me. I need you to learn to love Me first, before anyone else in your life, because I am going to use you." It was at this time that I received my probably my second or third revelation that I would preach and teach God's word one day. He went on to tell me that if my marriage of, at that time, seventeen years had gone through when I had my mother, my sister and my brothers to lean on, I would have ran. So He spoke clearly to me, "It is I, God, that has taken your perfect world and your perfect marriage and torn it down." I was not happy with that, but I was satisfied with it, because just knowing if God allowed it and caused it, then I could muster the strength to stand it.

He then took me to a scripture that would change my world and see me through all of this. In reading these passages, I gained a strength that surpasses understanding because the revelation and wisdom of God poured on my spirit like I had never felt before.

The end of a matter is better than its beginning and patience is better than pride. Do not be quickly provoked in your spirit, for anger resides in the lap of fools. Do not say, "Why were the old days better than these?" For it is not wise to ask such questions.
(Ecclesiastes 7: 8 -10)

These passages set me free from so much of my pain, but as I read on, God spoke loud and clear. "It's me. Rest."

Consider what God has done: Who can straighten what God has made crooked? When times are good, be happy; but when times are bad, consider: God has made one as well as the other. Therefore, a man cannot discover anything about his future.
(Ecclesiastes 7: 13 – 14)

As time went by, God began to take me to scriptures in the book of Proverbs, which taught about the adulterous woman and her plans and skills of seduction. I learned about the man who leaves his home and goes on a journey. I began to be lead to I and II Corinthians and James. So much teaching, and I knew it was the Holy Spirit guiding me and teaching me everything I needed to know to get through all of this. I began praying and having visions of a better future. I began journaling.

One night, I dreamed that I came upon my husband's car on Highway 285 here in Atlanta, and there he sat in the middle of the highway, stopped. His license tag was strange, because it had no number. I pulled up beside him and he was asleep and intoxicated. I pulled him from his car to mine, and he murmured his complaints against God. I took him to the church, and I took him to the basement of the church, and there Jesus sat at a long table with his twelve disciples. I laid him on the table and as he continued to murmur his complaints, I attempted to explain to Jesus all that was wrong in his life and what he was trying to say. Jesus spoke clearly to me to be quiet. He said to me, "I know everything wrong in his life. I know everything that has ever been wrong. I know what he suffered as a child, and I know what he suffers through as an adult. I hear him clearly. You don't." Jesus instructed me to go upstairs to the sanctuary and pray and that he would take care of Myke, and when I looked up and looked again at Myke where Jesus had him laying on the table, I only saw a basketful of rotten fruit. As I began to question Jesus, He put his finger over his mouth as to quiet me and reminded me again to go to the sanctuary and pray for my husband. He said as I walked away, "When I give him back to you, his fruit will be ripe." This was in July of 1994.

Wives, after this encounter with Jesus, I became a fool for Christ. I prayed like never before. I worshipped, I danced, and I shouted. I attended revivals and conferences in and out of the Atlanta area, and when people asked me in church where my husband was, I would always say, "He will be here." This attack on my marriage lasted until 1999, until we joined our present church.

Sometime about three years into all of this, as I became weary, I remember Elder Morton came to preach at the church I attended then, and she preached a sermon entitled, "Your Blessing Is in the Thicket." That woman's message from God loosed every chain, and every reasonable doubt that Satan had begun to replant in my mind that my husband was lost and would never be saved. It filled me with the Holy Ghost as Jesus had promised me. I thank her for that, and I have since then been to Elder Morton's church in New Orleans and verbally thanked her, but I am sure she does not remember, as when God is using you to heal in a mighty way like that, you basically bless many by just letting God use you at his will. As Elder Morton taught about Abraham taking Isaac up to the mountain as a sacrificial offering and trusting God, I was reminded of everything that Jesus had promised me, and that sermon gave me strength to go on for two more years as I listened to it daily. All my strength from the years of 1994 to 1999, until my husband really accepted Christ, I received from Christ.

Wives, listen to me and if you don't ever hear me say another word, hear this…. Stop talking to everyone about your marital problems and various situations. No one can help you get through this except Jesus Christ.

And only Jesus can help you understand and get through these times when it is tough in your marriage. This thing in my marriage seemed to have come from no where. This attack came so swiftly, and hit me so severely, that in my mind I lost balance and after a few conversations with people, as I said earlier, I immediately knew only Jesus was going to be able to see me through this.

When this attack hit my marriage, I learned in those years that it was only Jesus sustaining me, and that is why there is "The Married Women of Virtue" support group and this book, because God placed a charge on my life to give all that He poured into me, to help me sustain and stay lifted in those years, back to you.

There was specifically a chapter in the book of Proverbs written by Solomon, and three scriptures that helped pulled me through. I said it was the Bible and the scriptures that pulled me through, not my friends, not my family and certainly not my mouth. So once again, I want to teach scripture, because Jesus is tired of preachers and teachers who say they are called by Him to just keep talking and not teaching scripture, and that is why you will notice that I always back up what I say with scripture, because it's God's way. Without it, what I say should mean nothing to you.

The first scripture I want you to study is found in John 8:43- 44; this scripture will teach us that the unsaved cannot hear God's voice. Wives, stop badgering and yelling at your unsaved spouses about Christ and all He can do in the marriage to change things. Let God change you and teach you to be humble-spirited and quiet as you are instructed in I Peter 3:1. This scripture in I Peter teaches wives that it was the character of the wives that won husbands over in the Holy days, not their words. Your husbands cannot see the wrong in their lives and their feeling is that the biggest problem in the marriage is you. Guess what? At a certain point it is, because you won't be quiet and let God have His way with the husband.

> *Why is my language not clear to you? Because you are unable to hear what I say. You belong to your father the devil, and you want to carry out your father's desire. He was a murderer from the beginning, not holding the truth, for there is no truth in him. When he lies, he speaks his native language, for he is a liar and the father of lies.*
> *(John 8:43- 44)*

I love the next text of scripture because it teaches us again that Jesus is sitting at the right side of God, interceding on your behalf. You don't need to say a word.

> *You ask, "Why?" It is because the Lord is acting as the witness between you and the wife of your youth, because you have broken faith with her, though she is your partner the wife of your marriage covenant.*
> *(Malichi 2:14-16)*

Ladies, in marriage, Satan uses two strongholds that prevent us from living holy in our Christian marriages. I want to talk about those in this chapter because they are the two that are holding many of us back from being successful in our marriages, because we don't understand them scripturally and we don't understand how to fight against them in God's power.

They are: Anxiety (fear) and Unforgiveness.

Both words have so much power that I really did not know which one to begin with, but when I was going through the troubled times in my marriage, I asked God to teach me how to trust my husband and how to forgive, and these are some letters I wrote to myself that I want to share with you. They strengthened and they encouraged me.

> *Anxiety (fear)*   *04-15-95*
> *I am sure your first thoughts are, "I am not afraid."*
> *Well, if you don't trust God to deliver you and your*
> *husband from the circumstances in your marriage,*
> *then it is fear.*

No matter how you slice it up, anxiety is an unknown fear. Whenever something is out of one's control, the individual has to decide how he is going to play it. But just because the Christian has decided to trust God does not mean that the person will be totally fearless. In difficult circumstances, it is impossible not to have some doubts and accompanying fears. However, it is one thing to have fear and another thing to dwell on the doubts. It is at this time that you must not listen to satanic lies; instead, cast all your anxieties on the Lord because He cares for you.

Most Christians know this verse, and know they need to give their fear to God, but what they don't realize is that it is a process of giving Him the fear over and over again. Sometimes many times in the same day.

It is at this time that Satan will always try to undermine your faith, and cause the doubt to continually cross your mind. This is not due to a lack of faith. Listen to me! It is due to the relentless assault of the power of darkness. But even as God's peace stands guard over our hearts and minds when satanic forces attack in the form of accusations and lies, there will be turmoil as the battle rages until the Christian refuses to listen anymore, gives his anxiety to God, and moves on in positive thinking and actions.

But how! Because the next phase is getting past the hurt. And in order to get past the hurt, you must forgive, and how can you forgive someone who continues to hurt you, or has hurt you so much until you cant forget? This is where you have to learn to be Holy in your new Christian walk.... Only holiness can help you forgive and see the circumstances through the eyes and with the heart of Christ. You see, many Christians realize that forgiving is the thing to do. But they still struggle with forgiveness. A lot of Christians think they have forgiven someone who has hurt them, but they continue to struggle with the anger, distrust, recurring memories, and deep pain. So much so that they wonder what forgiveness is all about.

Forgiveness is a conscious decision not to hold something against someone who has hurt or offended us. This also means it is a decision to no longer be angry with that person. Forgiveness means to resolve to live with consequences of another person's sin. Forgiveness does not mean we no longer hurt when we remember what was done to us. In fact, we will still feel great pain for quite sometime. And when we see the offender, the forgiven person, or think about what the individual did, we may continue to feel emotional pain until we actually see God using it for Good in our lives.... Just because you still hurt does not mean you have not forgiven, but if you still feel anger when you see this person, you have not forgiven. So just because you still remember and still hurt, does not mean you have not forgiven.

The issue is anger. If you are still angry with that person, you have not forgiven. Possibly at this point, you realize that you are not angry because this person sinned against you, but you are angry because you cannot trust this person anymore.

Now does this lack of trust mean you have not forgiven? Let me share with you that forgiveness does not mean that you must tolerate

CINDERELLA, YOU LIED TO ME.

sin. Forgiveness does not mean that you are willing to be another person's doormat for continual sin. While it is okay to forgive past sin, you must begin to make some changes that will say. "I will not be a doormat for continual sin." We cannot keep ourselves in a position to be continually hurt again.

Forgiveness means, "I will not hold the past against you, but trust means you must show me you are not going to hurt me again." Matthew 18:21 reminds us that we should forgive endlessly, as we are forgiven by God.

We should never take on our own revenge, for the word says vengeance is the Lord's. So do not attempt to overcome evil with evil, but overcome evil with good; this is what brings forth true healing. In order to move closer to wholeness in this life, we need to realize that God only does what is good for us and best for us....

But how is this good? How can this pain be good? How can this suffering be good...? Because it causes you to take on the spirit of Christ, and when you take on the spirit of Christ, you take on the mind of Christ.

Let me remind you again what Ecclesiastes is stating to us. It begins by stating, "The end of a matter is better than the beginning." And when I read that in the midst of my marriage troubles, I couldn't digest that from God's word, because it made no sense. I never seen it coming, so I couldn't figure out the beginning of the matter, but it soon began to give me hope. I soon began realizing in this text that God had all of my problems in his hands and that it was all going to work out, because this scripture had a promise. Verse 10 went on to tell me that I shouldn't be saying, "Why were the Old Days better than these?" That blew my mind because all I kept saying was, "How could this happen after seventeen happy years? How could my marriage turn into sheer turmoil?" I had said that to myself so often. How much clearer could God make this for me? As I went on to Verses 13-14, I was set free. It went on to read that I should consider what *God* has done. Who can make straight what *God* has made crooked? It reminded me that in good times, I should be happy, but when times were bad, I should consider that *God, has made one as well as the other.* And that I could not discover anything about my future.

You know what, wives? It was this text in Ecclesiastes that helped me endure and never lose faith in knowing that all my marriage was suffering that God not only allowed it, but would see me through it. I was set free at that point. I was set free from worry, I was set free from pain, and I was set free from guilt and doubt that God would move on my behalf.

Wives, I am sure as I continue in writing this book that the devil would be pleased if I would finish right now and never write or speak another word to wives. But praise God, I am obedient to the voice of God and not the devil, the enemy. Yes, he is your enemy and the sooner you understand the fullness of what that means, the better you will be able to fight for your marriages. Don't let the enemy think he is your friend, and don't play patty-cake with him, don't entertain him, and don't even allow his strongholds to linger in your home. Exterminate and terminate his spirits immediately. He is a spirit of confusion, self doubt, distrust, division, separation and hell. His goal is to burden your heart with disbelief of God's word and take over your mind to operate in your marriage in the instruction and ways of this world. I understand that some of us who may be reading this book have already divorced and some of us may be lawyers or counselors who assist those divorced, by the Power of God, I have come to take away some of your business, because many marriages have ended in divorce and did not have to. Women especially have stood on everything else except for the word and promises of God.

Let me explain. In December of 2002, we held a revival at our church in Stone Mountain, Georgia, which ministered to the heart of the women. I followed the conference up with a class where I discussed the issues that we allow the enemy to store in our hearts. You see, we should only give our hearts to Christ. I have said that earlier in this book and I will continue to say it until you get it.

Your heart should be a place of peace, and if your heart is not a place of peace, then it must be a place of Hell. I like to call Satan out for who he is. I like to let him know he has been identified so we can expose him. That's why he struggles and fights with me daily. He hates me and I hate him, and he knows I am not afraid to reveal him, especially as it relates to the healing of marriages. By the power of God in me, he is defeated.

Anyway, one of the ministers who spoke at the conference brought out a point that we all have something stored in our hearts. She said it's a place where we store things. Well, God ministered to me that for some of us, we store things in this place deeply and we have small compartments where we keep our pains and hurts. For some of us, the pains are so bad we don't even dare go in to look unless we have some new hurt to put in there. Even then, we do it quickly after holding it awhile and crying over it for a few days. We like to keep it all separated, though, in its own compartment of the case. You see, in these compartments we have stored away old family hurt, old friend betrayals, pain our children caused, co-worker discouragement and such. All neatly stored in that private place, God's place, the heart. How dangerous? What a deception? My question to you, wives, is what kind of pain do we have buried so deep in the heart that we ourselves don't even like to go in and look at? What type of unforgiveness is buried there? What type of anguish and anger is buried there? Why do we carry this load in our hearts that cause us to walk around feeling sad, belittled, burdened, guilty, and useless? Yet we think because it is so deeply buried, that it is hidden, and still it shows in our eyes, and we try to make others think we are okay.

Have you ever looked at someone and you can see the pain in their eyes? Have you ever looked into someone's eyes and said, "That person looks like they have a broken heart"? Do you realize the magnitude of what has just been revealed to you at that thought? Have you ever seen someone hurting and you said, "Wow, my heart goes out to her"? Again, I say because spiritually we can see that her heart is full of the burdens she is carrying and she needs more heart, more heart space.

My point in this chapter is that if your heart is burdened with the cares of your marriage, and you're unable to forgive, then Satan has deceived you. You cannot carry pain and unforgiveness in your heart. Your heart is truly the only part of the body that belongs to God. It is the only part He will examine at your time of death and if He finds the suicidal thoughts, the hatred, the unforgiveness, the anger, the malice, the lack of distrust for him in it, you will not be able to get into heaven. The heart belongs to God and you must pray that God frees you and show you how to let go of all that you desire from man and begin to desire Him. You will know God has taken over your heart when you have a feeling of peace and joy, comfort and safety. Peace is a freedom from disturbance or disorder, and harmony; an undisturbed state of mind and that is what I want you to gain by reading this chapter. I want your mind to become free of the war.

I have explained to you that we cannot experience this kind of life when we allow Satan to store this Hell in our hearts; it is another plan of deception that keeps us from having a right relationship with Christ. It causes the life to be pressed right out of us. At this point, he begins to cause a depression in us. When he gets us to this point, he makes many begin to play the "what if?" game. "What if I were not here?" "What if I left him?" "What if I left him and the kids?" "What if I were dead?" Yes, I have counseled it ladies, and it gets this deep for many. Because this is the level of lowness he wants to take you to, and I advise you if you are at this level of lowness, to seek some Godly counseling immediately. Don't let Satan cause you to carry so much in your heart that it wears you down. Remember when the heart stops beating, life is over.

You see, wives, the bottom line and the ultimate goal of Satan is to destroy you and that is why we have to release those things we have stored in our hearts over to God. When you let that out of your heart, your mind is set free and you can think like Christ, and take on the mind of Christ, and the Spirit of Christ, and the heart of Christ.

In the end, all that will matter is when Christ reports the final condition of your heart to God.

If thou shalt confess with thy mouth the Lord Jesus,
and shalt believe in thine heart that God hath raised
him from the dead, thou shalt be saved.
(Romans 10: 9)

You can then begin to "Stand on The Promises of God." My husband, Myke, has accepted Jesus Christ as His Lord and Personal Savior. He not only attends worship every Sunday and Bible Study on every Tuesday, but he serves God in our church as the Senior Pastor's Armor Bearer, traveling with Him to serve as requested, he serves as a deacon and an usher. This is the power of a praying wife whose faith did not faint and did not fail. I tell you today, wives, that only this type of faith will cause you to stand of the promises of God. Don't ever believe in what God can't do in your marriage, always trust in what He can do. Just as He raised Lazurus from the dead, He can bring life back to your marriage when it dies. *Don't ever give up on God!*

The Real View of the Construction Site

The real view of the construction site. I am sure you are saying to yourself, "What in the world is she talking about now?"

When I think of the word marriage and I think about what the most important part of a marriage is, it leads me to talk about the foundation. First allow me to cover some other key factors in marriage and I promise I will get back to the construction site and make this all fit together.

This chapter is so important in helping you to understand the importance of a strong foundation in your marriage. I need to point out that a strong foundation in your marriage begins long before you are actually married. You see, many of us, whether we realize it or not, begin to establish foundations with our mates long before we even thought of getting married. Fortunately some of those foundations begin to crack, separate and weaken before the relationship can get off the ground and the relationship, somewhat like a child that would be born disfigured, terminates before any further birthing can take place. Unfortunately some of us press on and pursue in relationships that show all the signs of weakening and cracks in the foundation.

Before I go any further, I first want to give you a clear understanding of what the word "foundation" means as it pertains to marriage because we all have different styles of learning and we grasp subject areas differently. I want to be clear in my teaching. The word foundation describes the base of the Holy Institution we are building for Christ, ourselves and for others to be sitting upon. The base must be solid, smooth, sturdy, without many wrinkles, folds creases or dips. Its contents must be refined and free of impurities; poured and distributed evenly. It must have the width to cover all you will place on it and the depth to stand and hold firmly through all of the pressure and weight which will be piled upon it. If all of the standards described are not established within the foundation as described, at one point the foundation will begin to separate, weaken and crack. If the weakened foundation does not totally cause what is standing on it to fall, it will definitely never be able to withstand the pressures which will be applied and what is built on it will always have to fight to keep standing, because the foundation was not formed wide enough or deep enough.

This foundation can be thought of and used in many areas of what can be built—businesses, ministries, schools, houses and such—but the foundation we want to talk about concerns the foundation of marriage between two people.

Let me tell you where the foundation really starts. It starts when you first meet and you begin to get to know one another. You talk, you walk together, you laugh, and you share. This is a good start; this begins the refining process. It makes you care, it makes you share and eventually it will solidify and allow God to begin removing the impurities in the sand. It allows you, as a couple, time to discuss the differences you may have and see how you handle adversities and differences in opinion.

Unfortunately what happens during this point in a lot of relationships is that even when we see this part of the process is not working, we press on and keep moving in the relationship, because we want to be able to say we have someone special in our lives. This is one of the first mistakes many of us have made in the beginning of our relationships.

Next, we get refined and we make it through the initial process. A few rocks and pebbles remain, but we figure we can lay a pretty good foundation. Next is when many of us have messed up and stepped out

CINDERELLA, YOU LIED TO ME.

of God's will. Before God can get his hand in this "refined sand," as I
will call it, and wet it down for mixing, we move ahead of the plan,
begin lusting after one another and having sex, way before time, and
we are barely out of the initial process. Now guess what? We have
caused lumps to form in the refined sand along with the pebbles and
rocks that were already there. Now we have caused our sand to
contain many impurities.

However, we keep moving on, we keep pressing in this
relationship, which has now become a relationship of lust. And we
lust after each other more and more, never befriending each other ,
only lusting and desiring to be sexually responsive to each other. This
causes more and more impurities to form in the sand.

The next part to establishing your foundation is mixing it. You
have prayed and you have asked God to wet and mix this lumpy,
stony, impure sand together so you can lay your foundation and begin
to build, and God, being the loving God that He is, does just that at
your request.

So as He mixes, you disregard the hateful words you said to one
another, you disregard the rage, erratic behavior, lies, deceit, distrust
and disappointments you have seen in one another, and you press
forward.

(Keep in mind, this chapter does not address all marriages, this
chapter addresses couples who run into early disappointments with
one another. This chapter is intended to help couples understand
why they run into years of discontentment with one another and feel
like their marriage is hopeless.)

Soon after your foundation is poured, you are pleased and you are
planning marriage. Once you begin planning marriage, you are saying
to God, "We trust that you have taken our sand, wet it, mixed it,
poured it, and our foundation is ready to build on." At this point,
some couples have a good solid foundation and are ready for the
building process, but many do not and are not ready to place much
weight on this foundation. I say that because some of us asked God to
bless something that was unholy and filled with the garbage of this
world. Sin, lust, lies, and fornication.

73

We go to the builder now that our foundations are poured, and we ask him to show us our future. He brings out the blueprints and begins to show us a view of what the finished plans will look like, and it is beautiful, and we're happy. We begin to see visions of trim around the doors, the beautiful shutters on the windows, the green grass, the healthy shrubbery, flower garden, kids in the swimming pool and even a white picket fence and a decorated mailbox. We immediately begin to shop for the décor which will go inside of this house and we take note of the gold fixtures, the island in the kitchen, the full-size bathroom, the walk-in closets, and we tell the builder "yes" with excitement, "keep on building." We never look back to question the builder about the cracks and lumps we noticed that had begun forming in the foundation as the weight began to multiply.

The point I am making is similar to the point I tried to make in a communication class I taught for couples which is that we come into marriage with so many different ideals that we tend to overlook the smallest forms of mis-communication in areas that will later grow into larger forms of mis-communication until we miss God. We never seek pre marital counseling to smooth out some of this stuff and remove some of these pebbles and lumps that have begun to form. The sad part is that even when we do seek counseling, we don't stay with it long enough for it to make a difference. The reason this happens is that, many times, by the time we seek counseling we have already made so many other wedding preparations until we feel the sin is to turn back and let so many other people, who are not making a lifetime commitment to one another, down.

Here is what we need to understand. In I Corinthians 7:8 we are reminded that it is really better to stay unmarried. Could this be because God knew our lust and worldly desires would cause us to sin against one another? Did God know that our lust and worldly desires would cause us to build on weakened foundations? Did He know many of our marriages would be unhappy ones because we would not seek him on every hand?

And what is the reason that we push for marriage in spite of the lumps and impurities? What is the reason we keep moving forward when the counselor tells us to slow down and get to know one another better, or work through some difficult issues first? Could it be because we have already purchased the rings and set the wedding date? Could it be because invitations have been mailed to family and friends, and the announcement is in the newspaper? Could it be because we have hired the caterers and purchased our gowns? Why do we press and force ourselves to make a quick decision about the rest of our lives? Could it be because we're in love, or afraid we will never find love again?

Anyway, we tell the builder to keep building and make our dreams come true. We tell the builder to hurry, time is winding down, and the builder begins to warn us and tell us certain parts of the preparation of the house cannot be rushed. We miss completely that the builder who is telling us, "Slow down. You have cracks. You have lumps. You have pebbles." The builder is none other than Jesus Christ. He is saying to you, "Let's go back and repair this foundation now before we put too much more weight on it. Let's go back and repair some of those cracks. It's too weak to carry all of the burdens that will come with marriage. It's not wide enough to carry all of the stress and trials which will come against this marriage."

God says to you, "He doesn't speak to you right," and you say, "Oh, I will change him." God says, "You are not submissive enough to him," and you say, "Oh, I will change after we are married." God says, "He doesn't take care of his children from a previous marriage," and you say, "Oh, he will take care of ours." God says, "He doesn't believe in me and he doesn't attend church," and you say, "Oh, my pastor is good, I will get him going."

Excuse after excuse and you totally disregard the voice of God and keep pressing on. So could all your pain and suffering in this marriage be because of your disobedience? Could it be that you had an answer for everything? Could it be you just did not want to hear or heed God's voice?

The big day is finally here. The wedding is today. You're nervous, he's nervous and there you stand in the sight of God, ready to take these vows. Neither of you a member of this church; Grandma picked it out because this preacher sings well. It could be that your pastor would not marry you because you wouldn't complete premarital counseling. Maybe you just went to the courthouse to stand in front of a justice of the peace. You could just be keeping it as simple and as cost-effective as possible.

Anyway, now you are married. You stood in the sight of God and vowed to God, vowed to a Holy Institution ordained by God, and that is why it has become hard for you. Because you didn't understand that because this is a Holy Institution ordained by God, you cannot live it according to the world's standards. Listen, because you have taken a Holy Institution and attempted to live it according to the world's standard, it has become increasingly harder to have this marriage blessed. Now hear me! You may have blessings such as cars and wealth, but you are not happy. You have no joy, peace, or love for one another. You are simply rich and miserable. Again, you stood in the sight of God and you made a vow to God. The preacher stated, "We are gathered here today in the sight of God, to witness this man and this woman being joined in Holy Matrimony." He goes on to ask, "Is there anyone here who knows of just cause why this man and this woman should not be joined together?" You knew of just cause and you said not a word. Now here you sit some five, seven, nine years later, back in the counselor's office or in the office of the preacher who married you and you're wondering what went wrong. "Where did we go wrong?" "How did we miss it?" "Why is there no peace in my home?" "Why are my children unhappy?" "Why do we argue constantly?" And, somewhere deep in your mind, you feel like God has failed you. You feel like God is wrong for not stepping into this terrible marriage. You feel like God is wrong for not answering your prayers.

You say to yourself, "I am going to church, I am tithing, I am worshipping you, Lord. All I ask is that you come into my home and change things. I realize I have not done everything perfect, so I am praying that you will fix and change things." "What happened to the pretty view from the windows?" "What happened to the flower garden and the border and the white picket fence?" "Oh, God, it is like the harder I pray, the worse it gets." "We're growing further and further apart, Lord, where are you?" No answer. You have cried, you have prayed, you have fasted, and no answer.

Let me ask you, did one of the legs in the support system hit a crack in the foundation? Was the pressure that applied to the marriage so heavy that one of the lumps in the foundation burst and caused the whole house to weaken? Did you build your marriage on a foundation that was not ready for the pressures that come with marriage? You begin to search the Bible for scriptures to help you through this. You wonder why a merciful God has not stepped in. You read:

*Hear my voice when I call. Lord; be merciful unto me
and answer me. Do not hide your face from me, do
not turn away in anger; you have been my helper. Do
not reject me or forsake me, O God my Savior.
(Psalms 27: 7, 9)*

You cry and pray and it is with a total lack of understanding and all that is happening in your marriage just doesn't make sense. It just doesn't make sense. This man is acting as though he has lost his mind, and the harder you pray, the worse he gets. "Lord, have mercy, I think this marriage is over." "I can't take anymore."

Welcome to the real view of the Construction Site.

I said, "Welcome to the real view of the Construction Site." Wives, dry your eyes and listen. You have prayed and you have cried for God to step in and change your circumstances and change your home; make your house a home. And God has quietly stepped in to answer your prayers.

My words of wisdom to you:

Realize:

Realize who you have prayed to and begin to study your Bible everyday, so that you may gain the strength and wisdom of God. You are going to have to humble yourself under God's mighty hand and accept the authority of first God and then your husband like never before. You are going to have to obey this word. If you do not, you will not be able to stand against the attacks of the enemy which will come to try and test you during this difficult time.

Remember:

Remember that God's ways are not your ways. He doesn't see it like you see it, and He doesn't think about matters as you think about them, so what you see is completely different that what He is doing.

Recognize:

Recognize that you have just declared war against the enemy and you have told him you want your joy back, your peace back, your husband, and your home back.

Retaliate:

Retaliate against every attack of the enemy with the word of God, the peace of God, the understanding of God and the knowledge of God.

Roll:

Roll out the crazy faith. Because in order to get this breakthrough in your marriage, in order to get past every obstacle that will try you at this point, you are going to have to have crazy faith in God.

Rotate:

Rotate your role in your home from the dictator and ruler and submit it all to God and your husband.

Review:

Review the blueprints originally given to you and take note of all the cracks in the original foundation and understand completely that if you truly desire for God to rebuild this marriage, He will have to tear down to the original foundation. This means pulling flesh out of you and your husband until it hurts.

Remind:

Remind yourself of how dangerous a construction site really is. How dusty, dirty and blinding it really is when buildings and homes are being torn down. Think about how loud it is, and remember it never looks like the finished view until it is finished.

Relax:

Relax in knowing and trusting that your builder is Jesus, and He is a professional carpenter and knows how to work from the foundation. He knows how to clean things up after the hard part is finished. Know that God is not a fixer or a mender—that is "sissy" work to him. God is a builder, a Kingdom builder and if you truly desire a Kingdom life, you must allow him to tear Satan's kingdom, which you and your husband has built for yourselves, down. He is coming after worldly possessions, worldly morals, and worldly principles.

So wipe your eyes and dry your weeping tears. God is here. He never left you. You left him. He has seen your dreams and He has given you your plans, so He will surely bring them to pass if you would just hold on and never doubt. He has come to beat down the lumps and dig out the rocks and pebbles in the foundation that Satan allowed you to lay down and build your house on. It is not your spirit which cries, it is the enemy who causes you to cry, because he realizes that if he can keep you crying, he can continue to control you. He has seen the plans God has given you, and he knows God will bring them to pass, so he tricks you and makes you cry. He makes you cry because he realizes if he can keep you crying long enough, he can make you give up or worse.

When you stop crying, ask God to show you what you need to change in you to better your relationship with your spouse. When you stop crying, begin praying and don't ever give up on God. Remember that God will not rush this process. He will not rush this process because you shake your head in disbelief at what is happening all around you, and He will not rush this process because you threaten suicide. He will not rush this process because your bills are going unpaid. This is a view of the Construction Site. A Real View.

And why call ye me, Lord, Lord,
and do not do the things which I say?
(Luke 6:46)

Father, I pray now that you would move into homes across the nations and begin to tear down worldly foundations in marriages. I pray that you would begin to tug at the hearts of husbands and wives everywhere, pulling and digging out fleshly desires and pouring into them your spirit and power. I claim victory in homes right now as you rule and reign over hearts and minds. For each person who reads this book and prays this prayer with me, I claim victory, for we know our true blessing comes when we are able to pray for others in the midst of our own trials and tribulations. Wives, I pray your peace and strength now to endure any test which comes to try you. I pray you have an understanding and full revelation of seasons, God's timing and God's will for your life. I pray this complete prayer in the wonderful and mighty name of Jesus Christ. Amen.

Strong Woman of God, You Have Been Chosen

Many of us wonder why we walk so heavy as women of God, when we choose God and really begin to show a desire to walk in his will. We wonder why the load seems to get heavier and harder to carry and why the way seems so long. As we begin to pray more and pray longer, we come to realize that we become frustrated when what we see doesn't seem to be happening quick enough, and we begin to question God. Then the questions seem to move to our hearts and then our mouths, and then after that pattern completes its course, we become silent and the pattern begins again until we go around in another full circle.

As the trials become more severe and painful, we begin to verbally doubt this could be God at all who says He loves us everlasting. We wonder how a God with so much power could allow a pain to cut so deep and continue to last so long. So we begin to attend church more, and Bible study more, and special group revivals more. We begin to tithe, to pray, and give more of ourselves and our time. We join ministries where we can be free to serve more, and still things are getting worse. Some of us begin to say things like, "Wait a minute, God, I'm doing my part. I'm doing all you told me to do. I am obeying Your word. When are you going to step in?" And God is quiet, you hear nothing. No "yes," no "maybe," no "nothing," just no answer. You begin to feel like God is literally just a no-show in your life. *Just a no-show.*

You speak verbally again, "God, this is not fair, I've been doing well for weeks now, for months now, for years now, and nothing." "This is becoming unbearable, this is unbelievable and you've got to see the pain is thickening. Yet you won't step in. "

You scream, you shout, you doubt, you pout, you pull out your best tears, your best cry, your best scream of anguish and *still nothing*. Yet you listen over and over again to the pastors and ministers preach and the teachers of God teach, "God loves you and He will never leave or forsake you."

"God is a way maker. He is a company keeper, a friend in a time of trouble. He is a bright and morning star. He has plans to prosper you. Never get weary in your well-doing. He can heal your situation. He can feed you when you are hungry. He can quiet the storm. He turned water into wine. He raised Lazarus from the dead...."

All these miracles, all these blessings, and yet, in your situation, He has not stepped in, and it seems He won't and is not going to. You have the right to question God at this point. You are told by him to begin to repeat back to him all of his promises He made to you and you say, "Lord you healed all of these people in the Bible, you produced all of these miracles, you made all of these ways when a way was not seen for so many people, but you have not helped me, so where are you?" "The preachers keep telling me to hold on, hold out until my change comes, and I don't see my change coming. If it all were so simple, why have you not stepped in to heal my marriage and bless my home?" "Why? Why would you allow me to lose hope and give up?" "Why am I losing faith? I am almost ashamed to say that you know I am losing faith in you, Lord. I am really beginning to wonder if this will ever happen."

"Maybe there is a part of your word I am missing, maybe there is a part of your word that I missed that I didn't understand." "Maybe it is not meant for me to be married." "Maybe I am not meant to be happy." "Maybe I just married too fast. "Maybe I just married too young or too old." "Maybe marriage is not for me." "Maybe my marriage problems have just gone too far." "Maybe he was not the right man for me." "Maybe I am not the woman for him." "Maybe...."

"I mean, my girlfriends' husbands gave up their sin and straightened out their lives months ago. They now attend church together and both attend the support groups for married women at church. They are doing well. Maybe I am like my aunt, her husband left and never came back home. Things just never got better. Maybe I should cut the strings now and count this marriage a loss, let this man go and get on with my life. Oh, but how will I raise the children? I guess with alimony and child support, I can make it alone. Maybe I can get a part time job? Yeah that's what I will do, I can do this alone, I don't need a husband to be happy. I don't need a father to help me raise these kids. If this is what a Christian goes through, maybe I don't need God, I can just make it by myself. I don't need nothing or no one. I refuse to fight for this marriage another day, I refuse to be verbally insulted another day. It's too hard, it's unbearable, it's my life, and it's my decision. And that is the decision I choose to make this day, I am sticking to it. Now I feel better… It's clear and as much as this hurts, I am going to do it. I am tired of waiting on God to fix something that apparently cannot be fixed. I'll tell my friends and family in the morning. *Why should I fight another day?*"

"Because, Strong Woman of God – You Have Been Chosen."
You have been chosen in your family lineage by God for the purpose of building the Kingdom, chosen to help lead this generation to salvation and to a life with purpose for God. You, being a woman of courage, character, and charisma. A woman of strong moral and upright standards for Christ. To make a difference in this generation so that the next generation behind you can be blessed and know how to live and fight with God's strength and power to carry on. The Bible reminds us and talks about the foolish and wise builders:

> *Therefore everyone who hears these words of mine*
> *and puts them into practice is like a wise man who*
> *built his house on the rock. The rain came down the*
> *streams rose, and the winds blew and beat against*
> *the house; yet it did not fall because it had a*
> *foundation on the rock. But everyone who hears these*

words of mine and does not take them into practice is like
a foolish man who built his house on the sand. The rain
came down, the streams rose and the winds blew and beat
against the house, and it fell with a great crash.
(Matthew 7:24-27)

In Ephesians 1:11, we are reminded that we have been predestined by God according to the plan of He who works out everything in conformity with the purpose of his will. My point is that all of the pain and anguish I described that you go through in your marriages and in your homes is very, very minor in comparison to what Jesus came from heaven down to this world to suffer for us. Jesus was purposely sent here by God to be persecuted, to be laughed at, to be scorned, to face humility, and to die for us so that we might be saved. And we pray to him and we cry out to him to save us, and to deliver us, and free us from our pain and anguish, and He speaks to us. "My child, when you were in worship, you said you loved me and when you were on your knees, you said you loved me. When you got up, you said you understood why I came, why I died, and why I rose again."

Jesus speaks that you asked Him to make your married life better, you asked Him to make your family stronger, and He has come to answer your prayers. He's heard your words. He has heard your prayers. He has seen your tears. So He has chosen to you to bless…. But first you must be born again in His spirit. You continue to ask, "Why so much pain?" and He continues to say to you, "For this generation which I bring after you, you must be strong. You must be a Strong Woman of God, so I needed to test you. I needed to take you through the fire. I needed to try your spirit. I needed to see if you would die to your own flesh and personal desires. I needed to see if you were willing to suffer like I did even when there was no sign of the Father's hands being there to save you. I needed to see if you had truly taken on my spirit. It was the only way that I could know if you believed in me, had faith in me, and trusted me." Wives, God shared with me that He has so many blessings for you, so many gifts, and rewards for you, and the many generations that will come after you. But you had to receive Him.

CINDERELLA, YOU LIED TO ME.

You will be able to tell wonderful stories to your children
and grandchildren about the marvelous things I am doing
among the Egyptians to prove that I am the Lord.
(Exodus 10:2)

"And this is my covenant with them," says the Lord.
"My Spirit will not leave them, and neither will these
words I have given you. They will be on your lips and
on the lips of your children and your children's
children forever. I, the Lord, have spoken."
(Isaiah 59:21)

"You're going through your trials, and your test is the only way that you will receive me. And to receive me is to understand me. To understand me is to let me live in you. If I live in you, you must let me have life. If you let me have life in you, then you must imitate me. To imitate me, you must have my pains. To have my pains, you learn to endure in my pain. To endure in my pain, you become stronger. To become stronger, you must be persecuted. To endure persecution, you must be lied on. After you are lied on, you must be ridiculed and stoned. After you are ridiculed and stoned, you must learn to have joy and peace through it all. Through it all, your life has purpose. When you are purpose-driven for me, I can choose you. Once I choose you, I can begin to use you…. Strong Woman of God, You Have Been Chosen."

Before God uses you, He must know that you will not be hateful or angry. He must know that you will not act out of selfishness or evil ambition. He must know that you will not act out of vanity, or conceit. He must know you will not fight others, but you will fight for him, not in your own interest, but in his interest for others to be free. He must know that, through the storms in your marriage, you will be obedient. He must know that, even in your suffering, you will continue to pray. He must know that you will never give up on Him or the promises in His word. This is the only way, and God is the way.

This is what Jesus has spoken to wives who struggle with doubt, fear and ongoing disappointments. But many of you came to Jesus

85

because of your suffering, and you must realize that it was disobedience to God's word which has caused your suffering and it will be your sufferings that will bring you into obedience of this word. But then like Paul, even after you come into obedience, you will still continue to suffer because of your love for Christ. But now He knows you can and you will, because his Spirit has taken over your spirit and, like Paul, you have become a prisoner for Christ. Like Paul, you will begin to know that, through your prayers and the help given by the Spirit of Jesus Christ, what has happened to you will turn out for your deliverance. Paul's suffering was so intent and ongoing, I often wonder had it not been for his faith and belief and love for Jesus would He have made it through. Paul realized that he could not let his sufferings make him weaker and weaker, because if he had, he would not have been able to press on and preach this gospel.

His teaching lead masses of God's people to salvation. He realized his suffering was for generations to come. I said, his suffering was for generations to come. My question to you, "Where would you be if Jesus had allowed your sufferings make you more disobedient to God and become weaker instead of stronger?" For many of you, God placed this book in your hands at this appointed time so that you could become stronger and not weaker. In that I want you to become like Jesus and know your assignment in your family, and in your marriage. Take your focus off of your husband, your finances, and your problems and focus on Christ and his assignment and plan He has for you. What are your dreams for yourself? What are your plans? What are your visions? What does God want you to do for you today?

Could the problem be that, as wives, we don't understand our purpose? Maybe if we understood our purpose, we could get closer to Christ. Maybe if we understood our purpose, our children would be stronger, more reliable, more confident. Maybe if we understood our purpose, we could get through some of these tests without bringing the entire house down.

So you ask me:
How long is the test?
Exactly which part is the test?
How will I know if I am passing the test?

This is what God is looking for in many of you.

> *Therefore, my dear friends, as you have always*
> *obeyed—not only in my presence but now much more*
> *in my absence—continue to work out your salvation*
> *with fear and trembling, for it is God who works in*
> *you to will and act according to his purpose. Do*
> *everything without complaining or arguing so that*
> *you may become blameless and pure children of God*
> *without fault in a crooked and deprived generation,*
> *in which you shine like stars in the universe.*
> *(Phillipians 2: 12 -14)*

Wives, this is very specific instruction written in this text of scripture. Paul is leaving no room for ifs, ands or buts. He says that we should not just obey in His presence but in His absence as well. So does this mean that just because it has been several weeks and you have not received an answer from God, and you have seen no promises coming through, that you should start crying, cursing and giving up on the dream? Absolutely not. This is the time He is absent and He is watching you all the more. This means to me that not only should you treat your husband well at church and at the church picnic, but at home in private as well. This means God knows when we are being phony and acting for others.

You give out testimonies in church and to your friends and you tell about how wonderful, how loving Tommy is always meeting your needs, then you get home and curse Tommy out for not taking out the trash or bathing the children, or buying you a birthday gift…. God says, "Obey me in my presence, but in my absence as well." God wants you to realize that He not only resides in the church house, but in your house as well, and He is watching you. So you must always act according to God's purpose. Live your life in reverence to God, in trembling and in fear of God, everywhere you go, and in everything you do, that is the beginning of wisdom. Be filled with the Spirit of Jesus, be holy, and walk holy.

> *You were called to be Holy, just like the*
> *He who has called you is Holy.*
> *(I Peter 1:15)*

> *Humble yourselves therefore under God's mighty*
> *hand that He may lift you in due time. Cast all your*
> *fears on him because He cares for you.*
> *(I Peter 5: 6-7)*

Wives, stop yelling and preaching at your husbands, they cannot hear you.

> *Wives, in the same way, be submissive to your*
> *husbands, so that if any of them do not believe the*
> *word, they may be won over without words, by the*
> *behavior of their wives when they see the purity and*
> *reverence of your lives. For this is the way the holy*
> *women of the past who put their hope in God used to*
> *make themselves beautiful.*
> *(I Peter 3:1, 2, 5)*

Ladies, these words remind us that God wants us to blameless and pure, without fault. We cannot be that way if we are constantly focusing on our husbands and not on ourselves. We must learn to ask God to search us and show us what part we are playing in the downfall of this marriage, and we must be ready for the truth from God, for He will not lie when He shows you yourself. When He begins to show you yourself, then pray and ask him to lead and direct you in changing and follow the instruction that God gives you completely. You will know if it is God, because it will cut your flesh and you will doubt and fight with your flesh over the instruction, but you will not have peace in your spirit, because remember now that Christ controls your spirit. When you are out of God's will, you will not have peace, and the inner struggle, what your flesh desires to control and what the spirit desires to control will do battle.

Your husband should not be afraid to criticize you in fear that your temper will explode. God does not explode with us. He should be able to say to you when your dress is too short or your hair is not attractive. People should be able to look at you and say, "She has godly wisdom." This is why you have been chosen. God has a great purpose for your life. It was our Great Lord and Savior Jesus Christ that died for you. He died so that the works of the enemy could be destroyed in your life. He died so the diseases and genetic curses of divorce in your family line could be broken through you and your daughters and sons. He died for the sin your husband did against you. He died for the sin you committed against each other. So live, Strong Woman, live. You have been chosen, and you have victory through Jesus, The Christ.

The Truth About Cinderella

Who can find a virtuous woman? For her price is far above rubies. The heart of her husband doth safely trust her, so that he shall have no need of spoil. She will do him good and not evil all the days of her life.
(Proverbs 31: 10 – 12)

I want to talk about a character in this chapter that many of us grew up with, and I am sure we can relate to her. She is actually the theme and the inspiration for my book. Her name is Cinderella. How many of you know who Cinderella is? How many of you know her story and how she became one of the most sought-after women in a city? How many of you ever looked at Cinderella and asked yourself if she was a Christian with a strong faith, love and belief in Jesus Christ? I believe she was a Christian and she did believe in Jesus Christ. I know many of you never looked at Cinderella that way, because just as man planned when he wrote her story, he never intended for us to see Cinderella that way. But I looked at the story through my spiritual eyes, or should I say God's eyes.

This was one of my favorite stories when I was a girl, because like many of you, my desire was to become married and live happily ever after, just like so many other fictional characters. Cinderella's childhood in many ways was very similar to ours and her story was very much the same, yet I find God purposed her life to be married to a king, and in this chapter I will show you how.

I will show you in this chapter Cinderella's desire, her deeds, and her walk into destiny. I will show you how she desired the will of God to rule her life, and I will show you how her good deeds of servanthood caused her to walk in that plan of destiny God ordained for her life. True love, real love, good love, strong love—every little girl's fantasy. Man, what we would have done to have a man come along and with just one kiss, make all of our dreams come true? A knight in shining armor kiss you, and suddenly you're married and living happily ever after.

Happily ever after, that's the point of this book and that is where I want to keep my focus in this chapter. Because as little girls, and then young teenagers, and young women, we concentrate on the happily ever after. That is how many of us felt on our wedding days. We felt like this man, this husband we vowed to in the sight of God, would make all of our dreams come true and we too would live happily ever after. But was it? Were we prepared? I suggest that Cinderella was prepared for marriage. I suggest in her suffering she was being prepared, being prepared for a lifetime of happiness with a man she loved. We were not.

First of all, let me tell you about the heart and the spirit of Cinderella. She had love, she had joy, she had peace, she had meekness, she had goodness, she had gentleness, she had longsuffering, she had temperance, and most of all, she had faith.

Let me tell you what she didn't have. She didn't have anxiety about finding a man; she wasn't healing from a broken heart because of a past relationship. She had never experienced betrayal in a man. She wasn't bitter because of a man. She didn't have low self-esteem because of a verbally abusive man. And in spite of her circumstances, she knew how to love. She knew how to forgive. She didn't have a vindictive heart. She didn't have a jealous heart or spirit, even in spite of all that her evil stepmother and stepsisters put her through daily. The circumstances against Cinderella were great, but because of her desire to walk into destiny, she persevered. Cinderella had a Dad who was not in the home, a mother who this story never mentions, and she lived with a wicked stepmother and three wicked stepsisters. Still, in spite of all of that, she continued in her good deeds. She had the heart of a servant and the spirit of a servant and she served daily without complaint or murmuring. She did dishes, she cooked, she mopped, she scrubbed walls and floors, she sewed, and she did all of that for people who did not appreciate her, care about her, or in fact, even love her. Yet she continued to wait on God. She waited on God because of her desire for a good, happy and promised life.

She selects wool and flax and
works eagerly with her hands.
She sets about her work vigorously;
her arms are strong for her task.
(Proverbs 31: 13, 17)

And because of her faithfulness and trust, she was able to walk right into the plan of destiny God had lain out for her. One night, God sent her an angel who prepared an evening of beauty for her, who gave her instructions from the Master to obey and a time to be home. Unlike us, Cinderella was obedient to all of the instructions. Because of her obedience, because she followed all the instructions from the messenger of God, the angel whom God sent her way, Cinderella was blessed with a man honored in the Kingdom.

Her husband is respected at the city gate, where he
takes his seat among the elders of the land.
(Proverbs 31:23)

Cinderella did not run after this man who showed her affection at their first meeting. Cinderella did not sleep with this man on the first night she met him. Cinderella did not chase him down to give him her phone number, nor did she ask for his. Because of her holiness, the man fell in love, and came back to search the city far and wide for her until he found her. And when he found her, the story reminds us they lived happily ever after.

I suggest that Cinderella made a good wife. As I stated earlier, Cinderella had good morals and characteristics. I outlined for you the heart and spirit she did not have. Cinderella had a heart of love, even for her enemies, and she had been trained to be a helpmate and to have the heart of a helpmate.

*She gets up while it is still dark, she provides food for
her family and portions for her servant girls.
(Proverbs 31: 15)*

Is this passage suggesting that this woman, a woman like that of Cinderella, will even train her daughters to be servants? Servants whom God will be pleased with? She was honest, obedient to God and trusted by the angels sent to protect her. She had no need to prove herself to a man or be a whoremonger.

Cinderella did not enter her marriage possessing a lot of material pleasures; she was content with her present conditions as she waited on God. And she never let go of her dream that an angel sent from Heaven by God would one day honor her longsuffering, prayers, and obedience in the midst of being rejected by her Dad, left by her mother, and mistreated by her other family members. We never read where Cinderella walked away angry or ran to her room crying. We never read where she threw the mop down or sought revenge on her step family. We never read where she curses everyone out and leaves, slamming the door. We never see where she had suicidal thoughts because of the circumstances in her life. We only see where she continued to serve in obedience while waiting on the direction and plan of destiny to take place in her life.

Notice again, wives, this book never talks about Cinderella walking the streets at night lonely and dissatisfied, just looking for a man, any man, to comfort her and hold her tight. We don't see depression seeping in because she did not have a date. Again she just stood on her prayers and faith while waiting on God. I am trying to show you, strong women of God, that even when you feel like you are in a prison and the circumstances seem to become overwhelming, that God has a plan and a purpose. Cinderella waited on God, and she met a man who was so mesmerized by her goodness and purity that he wanted to marry her. He met her at a Grand Affair planned by God.

We never find out much about the prince in this story, we just know that he was rich, he was a gentleman, and he sought after a virtuous woman, a Kingdom woman, and God, being God, had prepared for him, from birth, Cinderella. Please take note that a virtuous woman does not have to go about bragging that she is a virtuous woman. Her light just shines before others because of the way she carries herself.

> *She is clothed with strength and dignity, she can laugh at the days to come. She speaks with wisdom, and faithful instruction is on her tongue. She is a lady at all times and she is constantly about her Father's business. She does not mistreat others even in her own sufferings.*
> *(Proverbs 31: 25, 26)*

> *Her husband has full confidence in her and lacks nothing of value. She opens her arms to the poor and extends her hands to the needy. She watches over the affairs of her household and does not eat the bread of idleness.*
> *(Proverbs 31: 11, 20, 27)*

These were the characteristics of Cinderella before marriage. I just said something and I will say it again. These were the characteristics of Cinderella *before* she got married, so when God came to bless her for what He had seen in her, she at first did not know the angel was a messenger sent by God. She had no idea it was her final testing before walking into God's plan of destiny. She had no idea this was a set up that would bless her for the rest of her life.

We know the angel who came was sent by God, because even the angel did not have Cinderella go out and spend money. She did not have on new clothes, makeup and hair, to impress a bunch of people Cinderella didn't even know. The angel suggested they take material from around the house and make it work miraculously for this occasion and Cinderella agreed.

*Your beauty should not come from outward adornment,
such as braided hair and the wearing of gold jewelry
and fine clothes. Instead, it should be that of your
inner self, the unfading beauty of a gentle and quiet
spirit which is of great worth in God's sight.*
(I Peter 3: 3, 4)

The angel transformed mice into strong white horses and changed a rat into a handsome driver for her. Does this show you God can do anything? He can even change the rats and mice in your life into servants for you. When Cinderella saw God produce all of these miracles, the story says she became so filled with excitement she thought she would burst. That was the Holy Spirit. After all God had moved into the circumstances of her life which kept her down and was showing off in all of his power. After all of that he presented her with, glass slippers to remind her of how fragile she was on this evening. He presented her with glass slippers as a reminder to stay obedient. He prepared them especially for her, especially for this evening. Would you say that is kind of like walking on eggshells?

The angel then gave her specific instructions from God that she must follow throughout the evening. I can imagine he told her that she would meet someone who would become very special to her, someone who would show her love and affection like she had never seen before, attention like she had never been shown before, not even from her father who had left her in horrible conditions. I am sure this angel told her that no matter how special this man made her feel, no matter how good the attention was, that she was not to make another date with him, she was not to chase after him, and she was not to give him her number. I am sure he reminded her that her focus for the evening was to have fun and remember God.

Sure enough, just as the angel had said, he was there, and they danced all night. But unlike many of you, Cinderella, in fear and reverence of God, obeyed every rule, right down to when the clock struck midnight. Cinderella never allowed any of this man's wooing separate from her the instructions of Christ. She heeded the instruction exactly as told by the angel and ran out of the ballroom at midnight. I can imagine the prince being as charming as he was, had never been turned down by any woman before, especially after pouring on such heavy charm as he had on that night. I am sure it was rare for him to meet a woman of this caliber and standards. What others in the room would have done to be with him, yet she runs out, kicks her way out of a glass slipper, a fragile slipper, that never cracks or breaks, and she never looks back.

I am sure he was in total astonishment. But I bet he said to himself, "That was a Kingdom woman, a virtuous woman, a Proverbs 31 woman. I will make her my wife, because a Kingdom man surely should marry a Kingdom woman." I bet the Prince tossed and turned all night wandering how he would ever find this woman who could possibly be fit to walk in such a fragile slipper. I can imagine he had plans to rise early in the morning, find her, and make her his wife.

A man who findeth a wife findeth a good thing and
has favor with the Lord.
(Proverbs 18: 22)

The prince knew this woman would make a good wife and cause him to have favor with the Lord, something he probably, in all his riches, had never had in his life. So he rose early the next morning and began searching the city for her, from town to town and from house to house. He looked all day at women's feet to find his bride. *Who,* he must have asked himself, *can be fit to walk in a glass slipper?* And finally, he came to the home of Cinderella and her evil stepsisters.

And again, as I stated earlier, God, being God, blessed her, and God blessed her right in the presence of her enemies who also desired this blessing. Then He kissed her, because he had not only found her, he loved her, and he desired for her to be his wife, so he asked her to marry him. They were married and the story ends by telling us that this couple was filled with joy and lived happily ever after.

The reason I am sharing this chapter with you entitled, "The Truth About Cinderella," is because so many wives have married with this Cinderella fantasy in mind, but as I stated earlier, they had the Cinderella fantasy but were not willing to complete the training before reigning. Therefore, many of you don't cook, you don't do laundry, you don't clean, you're not meek or submissive in your spirit, you're bitter, you're envious of others and you have a jealous spirit. Because of all of this in your spirit, Christ cannot live through you and bless you or your marriage the way you desire and the angel you have been waiting for will never come. Better put, the angel probably has come and you have put the angel out of your life, because you didn't recognize it when it was here.

We have too many married women with attitudes of self righteousness, and they only care for themselves. You want the man, but then when you get him you don't take care of him. You won't serve or sacrifice for him, because you feel life is unfair. Therefore, your happily ever after will never come. He will never be able to sit among the elders at the gate because you won't represent him well when he is not around; you talk about him and ridicule him to others at any given moment.

Wives, God fills us with the ability to be effective wives, mothers and business women if that is what we desire; however, in our hateful, spiteful, unkind and unloving ways in which we treat our husbands, we show God over and over again that we don't want the joy, peace and blessings he has for us in our marriages. We show God over and over again that we will not stand by this man, and much time, we won't even stand by our children, because they should not be unhappy. Yes, wives, mothers, children should not be unhappy. They have everything to live for, and you set the example. If your light is not shining, neither will your child's light be shining. Wife, if your light is not shining and your children's light is not shining, then most likely your husband's light will not be shining. Therefore, no one has the glory of God upon them and the house will not be living under a blessing, but under a curse.

Her children rise and call her blessed; her husband
also, and he praises her.
(Proverbs 31: 28)

Many of you with daughters, you take time to make sure thy leave you alone, but you don't take time to be alone with them. You don't teach them how to manage their weight or take care of their bodies properly, their feminine issues and needs go neglected and their hair is untamed. Their appearance is several notches below how well you keep yourself. Therefore, they are ridiculed and laughed at in school and their esteem is low or their behavior is not under control. Mother, wife, this starts with you.

We don't spend time alone with ours sons and daughters to talk with them about their feelings, their pains, and their anguishes while they are young, and then when they become teens, we let the world tell us there is a communication block. It is not a block, it is something that was never set in place, and you cannot block something that was never moving. We are losing our children every day to violence, gangs, suicide, drugs, sexually transmitted diseases (STDs) drinking and other ungodly tendencies, and we wonder where we failed. We failed because we succumbed to our own selfish desires and we didn't take the time out to talk, to love, to care, to discipline or to teach our children about the cycles of life and how God could step in and commission them, change them and challenge them.

As a woman and prophet of God and of great faith, I shared with you this story and revelation from Jesus Christ about Cinderella so you could see that God can step into any circumstance, it doesn't matter how bad, and cause a miracle in your life, in your home and within your family.... I also shared that your desire had to be for Christ, but your deeds had to be in order and in line with the word, and that is to always desire, no matter what the situation, to serve others. As a matter of fact, many of you need to change your prayer from what God can do for you to what can you do for others. You see, God is looking for people who want to serve other people and this is what Cinderella did with a right heart, mind, and spirit. I am convinced this is how she got her breakthrough and walked into destiny.

She allowed God to train her properly to care for a home, a family and a man, and this is what we must be willing to do for ourselves and our daughters—step, foster, legal by death, biological or otherwise.

It's not too late. This story shows us that by faith God will and can cause us to live happily ever after.

> *Give her the reward she has earned and let her works*
> *bring her praise at the city gate.*
> *(Proverbs 31:31)*

This is:
"The Truth About Cinderella"

Letters of Testimony and Love

Prophetess Adrienne,

Thank you very much for the encouraging words of wisdom. I have enjoyed your class so much. I tell all the married women on my job about the wonderful prophet God has sent my way. I know it can be a tough ministry, but we really need a strong sister like you to keep us straight. I will continue to pray for your strength every night. God bless you and please continue to pray for me.

Love Danita J.

Good morning Minister Swearingen,

I have been truly blessed by the Married Wives of Virtue. I have grown in that I have an understanding of my role as a helpmate. I have learned to totally rely on God and give everything to Him. I learned to focus and concentrate on me and ask God to fix me. It has helped me to give my heart, mind, and soul back to God, where they belonged in the first place. I had given so much to my husband that everything that happened to or with him consumed so much of me. I had lost myself. I have learned to be patient and wait on God, especially when I don't know what is happening or going on with my husband. I have learned not to always open my mouth and say what I want. By waiting on God, I feel so much better when I don't or even when I do say what He wants me to say. Because you know that sometimes God does want you to say some things that need to be said.

I revel in anointing my home and God filling it with the Holy Spirit, which wards away anything evil and not of God. My home is so peaceful and I am at peace with whatever happens in my marriage. I have learned that through prayer, faith, and totally giving everything to God, He will totally and completely take care of me. He has trusted me enough (little old me, unworthy me), to hear His voice. I now wait to hear from God, I try very hard not to make a move without first hearing from God. I know now what it feels like to know that God is ordering your steps. I am glad and truly blessed by this ministry. I thank God for Adrienne and Pastor Lee, because I was on the verge of giving up. I am trusting totally in God and standing on His promises. I now know that I can handle anything that comes. Before, I thought I couldn't or wouldn't make it if I didn't have my husband. I know that I can do and handle all things through Christ. I feel as though God sent this ministry especially for me at just the right time, taking care of me again as always.

Be Blessed!!!!!!!
Angela H

Minister Adrienne,

I just want to take moment to say thanks for your words of encouragement and for your prayers.... I feel so blessed.... I feel God has truly showed me favor.... My pregnancy test was positive last night I'm calling my doctor for an appointment today.... Again, thanks.... Faith-Fruitful and Favored, that's me.... To God I Give the Glory.... Amen!

Deborah

Prophetess Adrienne,

I was truly blessed at your licensing sermon. Words cannot express what you pour into my spirit *every time*. I am privileged to be under the sound of your voice. I have not, in all of my 32 years, ten months, and four days of existence, been in the presence of a woman of your caliber... let alone had the opportunity to receive instruction on what being (and in my case becoming) a woman really is all about.

I know it is not often that we greet and meet with one another, but you are in my thoughts and prayers daily. Prophetess, I am honored to know you not as a "scripture quoter" but a "scripture keeper." You, Prophetess, inspire me in ways that are too numerable to list. As I type this e-mail, please know my heart is oozing (full and overflowing) because only God himself knows the state I've been in (not only maritally).... He knew that you would be the one to reach and teach me.

My pastor tells us... find someone we admire and pattern ourselves after them... with admiration... with inspiration. I continue in prayer for the materialization of all the fruits of the holy spirit... the very fruits that are made manifest in your being... I must praise God for what He has done... what he is doing in your life.... I know the best has yet to come!!!!!!!!!!!!!!!!
Truly, Prophetess Adrienne, you are the epitome of a godly woman.... You are my hero! God bless you!

Jacqueline

Hi Minister Adrienne and Brother Mike!

I *enjoyed* our six-week class. Thanks for your time and your commitment to the class. It was a blessing for my marriage. It has helped both my husband and me to understand one another better and definitely understand God's plan for marriage.

I believe the seeds were planted for us to water and grow into a new foundation built on Christ in our marriage. Thank you for covering each and every marriage in prayer. My gratitude for your labor of love cannot be expressed enough. I pray that God pour blessing upon blessing upon blessing upon you and Brother Mike.

I also pray that God enlarge your territory and make room for your gift so that more marriages may be blessed by your ministry. Thanks again and God Bless!

Angelyn and Cedeno

Adrienne Swearingen,

The Lord has placed you in my life so that I can be a better person and to guide me in the right direction, you are truly a blessing.

Love Bonita P.

MinisterAdrienne,

In being in the MWOV classes, I realized I was not the wife God intended me to be, I was the wife that I thought I should be. I see how God is restoring me (first), so that I *will be* the godly wife He wants. God is showing me how to have *great peace* in spite of any marital circumstance. I have seen my marriage change from talk of divorce to talk of desire. From talk of what a good husband and a good wife should do, to talk of what a godly husband and a godly wife should Do. *Only God!!!* Adrienne, thank you for *teaching* me what a MWOV is. Thank you for teaching me that I can get as *craaaazy* as I want to get with my faith, and most of all, thank you for teaching me about the Construction Site. And I definitely want to thank God again for your awesome ministry.

Barb A.

Holy Matrimony Prophetic Ministries

I would like to offer my sincere and heartfelt thanks to you for supporting and being a blessing to this ministry. Words simply cannot express how I thank you for purchasing this book. If the Lord is willing, and I believe He is, this is only the first in a series of three books. Watch for my next two books in this series to be released very soon.

When The Vow Breaks, "Stand!"

From Bitter to Better, "Wives Defeating Satan"

God bless you,
Prophetess Adrienne Swearingen

If you would like to obtain information on
how to order additional copies of this book
for your church, family or friends,
send your name and address to my email:

HolyMPM@aol.com

You may also visit my website at
www.HolyMatrimonyPropheticMinistries.org